ZODIAC

NORTH CHESHIRE

Edited by Steve Twelvetree

First published in Great Britain in 2002 by
YOUNG WRITERS
Remus House,
Coltsfoot Drive,
Peterborough, PE2 9JX
Telephone (01733) 890066

HB ISBN 0 75433 542 9
SB ISBN 0 75433 543 7

FOREWORD

Young Writers was established in 1991 with the aim of promoting creative writing in children, to make reading and writing poetry fun.

Once again, this year proved to be a tremendous success with over 41,000 entries received nationwide.

The Zodiac competition has shown us the high standard of work and effort that children are capable of today. The competition has given us a vivid insight into the thoughts and experiences of today's younger generation. It is a reflection of the enthusiasm and creativity that teachers have injected into their pupils, and it shines clearly within this anthology.

The task of selecting poems was a difficult one, but nevertheless, an enjoyable experience. We hope you are as pleased with the final selection in *Zodiac North Cheshire* as we are.

CONTENTS

The Poems

AMERICAN APOCALYPSE

Internal flights, queuing at traffic lights
Going to see world famous sights
It started as a normal Tuesday morning
No one knew of the tragedy dawning

Four planes take off in different directions
These aircraft will be remembered for generations
All are hijacked by men bearing knives
Passengers are forced to ring their beloved wives

America loses all of its power
As one plane hits the North Trade Tower
A tragic accident costing many lives
But then the second plane fatally dives

The Pentagon is their next victim
George W Bush doesn't know what's hit him
Terrorists change the world in these few hours
As a huge fireball engulfs the twin towers

Desperately workers start jumping from the sky
Or ringing home to say goodbye
All of a sudden we hear a rumble
And the famous twin towers begin to crumble

And then the sight I will never forget
New York looks like fish in fishing net
Engulfed by smoke and clouds of dust
We will find who did this, we must, we must

One by one bodies are pulled from the rubble
Millions mourn and tempers bubble
Freedom and hope still lives on
Even when loved ones are dead and gone.

Vicky Howard (13)
Knutsford High School

IMAGINATION ISLAND

The day fades to dark
My daily jobs are done
I wander off into my dreams
Heading for a tropical sun.

The smooth silky sand greets me
The waves lap around my feet
I am heading for a dream adventure
My soulmate I will meet.

My feet lead to a clearing
A beach and dark green trees
Parrots soar above me
A breeze blows through the leaves.

The sun shines clear and brightly
The glare bathes on my face
It's wonderful to dream
In a hot, tropical place.

I'm walking through the forest now
My steps are quite unsure
For what I next will have to face
The sea or forest floor.

I can see quite clearly
The sight in front of me
A golden, tanned stranger
A friend or foe is he.

A native of my island
In my muddled world of dreams
Nothing is for certain
Nothing as it seems.

The alarm rings in my head
My dream is over, I'm out of bed.

Kayleigh Crompton (13)
Knutsford High School

MINDMAPS

Alone, abandoned, forgotten, housebound.
A love for travel destroyed.
Every day he sits studying his collection.
Maps piled high in every corner.
His legs can't carry him but his imagination can.
Across blisteringly hot deserts.
Surviving polar climates.
Touring humid rainforests.
Conquering mountain summits.
Exploring dead cities and civilisations.
Sailing wide oceans and travelling every road.
Meeting new people and scanning new faces.
Tasting exotic foods and seeing new sights.
Changing continents and crossing borders.
Trekking many countries and conquering every mile with ease.
And as his journey finishes
His image of youthful dreams turns to a mirage
And his pains of age return.
He sleeps, tired from the journeys of his mind.

Anna Beaumont (13)
Knutsford High School

The Roller Coaster

There it stands like a noble beast
Overlooking a park full of risk
Polished red tracks of twisted metal
Weave in and out of a monstrous cave
Full of secrets and surprises, unseen by the human eye
Long carts of metal allow passengers to board
It chatters up and up a long track that seems to lead to the heavens
Stops in mid-air and everything seems to be normal - too normal
Suddenly out of the blue
You plunge down a track leading to nowhere
The track makes sharp turns
Like a snake catching up with its prey
The speed is phenomenal
Ricocheting around the whole park
Violent turns and unbearably sickening loops that never end
Coloured blurs wrap around like some beast-like blanket that
Devours humans in a single effortless motion
It stops
And there is a feeling of sheer delight and relaxation
Which powers a sudden adrenaline rush
To battle the beast again!

Nick Denton (13)
Knutsford High School

The Wave's Storm

His heart thuds,
as the lonely wave seeks attention.
Climbing from the depths of his sapphire cage
foaming at the mouth, as he thunders down furiously.

He gasps for breath,
as his fury leaves the milky shore,
silent in his invisible muzzle,
as he clears the rugged hurdle.

He turns in fear.
Unleashed if only for a minute,
independent as the seagulls fly high above his brow,
he groans in relief.

Taking a further step,
he no longer groans in relief but only in fear,
sharp stones thrust at his wounded skin

The sea breathes no more!

Viv Bowdler
Knutsford High School

The World Lives On!

The Earth shook with a huge force,
Like a frightened lost boy,
Alien sulphur had surfaced,
As if looking for a toy.

The ground burst open and lava spilled out,
Like water spraying out of a fountain,
Large rivers of boiling red liquid,
Meandering down the old mountain.

Huge red fireballs,
Thrown from their gigantic dome,
Destroying un-collapsed buildings,
Randomly hitting a selected home.

The sky filled with rage,
Struck with an enormous, heavy blast,
Icy cold water poured down,
How long would the nightmare last?

Rebecca Millson (13)
Knutsford High School

THE PLAY OF LIFE

Life is like a theatrical production
Bringing out the best in all its cast,
Who, when not on stage
Are worthless, expressionless shells,
As though washed up on the lonely, lifeless shore of redundancy,
Left to wait for their next audition,
And another chance to live.

'Curtains up,'
The lights go dim,
Expectant silence fills the air.
And this, the start of a brand new life,
The actors are reborn.
The lively bustle of chaos,
The secret romance of the prince,
The ear-shattering screams of murdered kings,
The stage of life is filled with such emotion,
It never ceases to amaze.

Some actors take the lead roles,
Others, walk-on parts.
Everyone essential to life's story,
No less important than another.
And when at last the curtain falls,
The onlookers in life have finished their applause,
The characters are cast aside,
To join the long audition queues once more,
In the hope of living, for just one more play.

Johanne Stephenson (13)
Knutsford High School

Cold Coffee

The dusky light drifts in across the stained carpets,
It has no purpose but to glide lazily across the old man's tired face,
Tension claws at my stomach,
What will he be like after all this time?
I can't see him again,
I let my eyes slide down to the plastic coffee cup in my icy hands,
The glutinous liquid has turned stone cold as I wait,
My head is bursting with emotions,
After all this time I can't act like nothing's happened,
He won't remember me,
What am I doing here?
I stare around the bleak walls,
A loud snore echoes from the opposite bench,
An elderly man sleeps as his wife gravely reads
Endless trashy magazines with loneliness in her eyes,
Lifeless,
Grey,
They are all in a time warp,
Floating along aimlessly,
No one else looks nervous,
They barely seem to notice they are here,
I should leave,
'Flight 2091 has arrived at gate 4.'

Sarah Lawless (13)
Knutsford High School

The Gate Opener!

I put on the saddle and jumped up high
We galloped away like a cloud in the sky
To spur her on I had no need,
The wind pressed my face as we gathered speed
Over the bridges, up Veno hill,
Through the dark woods and past the old mill
Jumping the streams and over the ridges
Along the river and over the ditches,
Foam and sweat sprayed her back
But not for one second did she ever slack
The train turned to meet its fate
As I dismounted quickly and opened the gate
I let her eat grass as I sat down to rest
What would have happened if she hadn't done her best?
I dare not think about it
Phewwww.

Kimberley-Jo Cowell (13)
Knutsford High School

A Coral Jewel

Evening in Hawaii and the golden moon shines down.
Sooty black sand lies on the ground.
Girls wear flower chains,
You feel at ease with no pains.
Children splash in turquoise seas
Coconuts nestle in the trees.
A party dances in a golden ray
This carries on all through the day.
The glistening coral reef is all around,
Morning in Hawaii and the orange sun shines down.

Natalie Freeman
Knutsford High School

DROWNING

I sat there in fear, marvelling at its enormity,
Its power, pace, spooky to think of.
It has a mind you know.

It closes in on the shore. The sand under its feet.
It creeps and it crawls. Its hissing noise in the wind,
As it sways like a carpet, how dare you budge me.
It has a mind you know.

In day it slaps the shore, looks up, it'd never hurt me
It's beautiful. In the day. But it has a mind you know.

It swallows up the sun and in the failing light, silence
Spreads for it all starts at night.

Oops, silly me, it hypnotised me,
It won't let go, pulls me under,
Her coldness eats at me, I can't
Find the surface, she's disorientated me,
She has me. It has a mind you now.

Let me go, I plea, I'm at your mercy,
I toss and turn and clatter on the floor,
If only I could find my feet,
What a treat that would be.

I have to accept it, the solid surface
Is impenetrable. I can't break free.
My heart is racing, I can hear it, down here.
I gasp for air, it's only there, so close.

Wait! Everything's gone quiet.
I can't feel pain anymore.
What's happened?
It has a mind you know, the sea.

Warren Thompson (15)
Lowton High School

The Painting

He sits as if frozen
A droplet on a lonesome tree
He stares at you blindly
But he can see.

You relate to his sorrow
But his sorrow isn't shared
Like a freeze-frame of what was
As if just occurred.

You look on with curiosity
But the eyes are blank
He is trapped within the painting
Still waiting for that chance.

He dreams of wild horses
They will take his torture away
But this dream he has had for years now
Almost a century to the day!

Rebecca Hines (16)
Lowton High School

The Game

Wigan St Pat's,
That's who we play.
We shall win,
At the end of the day.

The whistle blows,
We kick to them.
They knock on,
Silly old men.

It's half-time now,
We're down by two.
We need help,
And it's going to come from you.

We've won the game,
Thanks to you.
The final score,
Is 22-2.

Chris Lane (13)
Lowton High School

WINTER

A carpet of snow awaits me,
    Not a single crease there,
The warmness in the house,
    The coldness remains,

Layers of clothes go on,
    The front door lingers open,
The coldness strikes me,
    I step out onto the snow,

Grasping a cluster of snow,
    I aim it at my friend,
'Bash' right on back,
    I score, that's one for me,

Reaching for more snow,
    On behalf of a snowman,
I turn towards my friend,
    'Bash' that's one a piece.

Hannah Johnson (13)
Lowton High School

Summer's Delight

Summer arrives only once every year,
This is the time when no one needs to shed a tear,
This is part of summer's delight.

You've got to enjoy it whilst you can,
So this year we've made out a plan,
This is part of summer's delight.

You can relax all day and all night,
If it goes cold it gives you a fright,
This is part of summer's delight.

You can never trust the summer sun,
So you have to have lots of fun,
This is part of summer's delight.

We're all sad to say goodbye
When summer goes I want to cry,
This is part of summer's delight.

Daniel Rogers (13)
Lowton High School

School

School is a prison,
Where you're locked up all day,
You have to do work,
And there's no time for play.

Some teachers are surly,
And some are a bore,
From time to time,
You'll hear students snore.

What most boys dream of,
When they're at school,
Is a bronzed bevy of blonde bathing beauties,
Basking blissfully beside a blue pool.

You work off a clock,
And you're ordered about,
If you're not as quiet as a mouse,
Then you'll be sent out.

Jonathan Morgan (13)
Lowton High School

Me

I am torn between love and hate,
Love for my mother,
And hatred for my stepfather,

After seeing what man is capable of,
I decide to live free,
Like the bird,
Making my own decisions,
Flying solo.

What I have seen will only make me a better person,
I will not let myself follow,
I will lead,
I shall shape my own life.

I am not here to follow footsteps,
I am here to make my own,
I am here to make an impression,
To show others who I am.

Marc Davies (15)
Lowton High School

MIDNIGHT

Dragons, witches, lost in the wood,
The girls were running as fast as they could.

Rats and spiders, a little mouse,
The girls were happy, they saw a house.

They stepped inside and began to fall,
They landed with a bump, they were in the hall.

Cobwebs, clocks and a missing stair,
The thing that stood was Lucy's hair.

Upstairs, downstairs, which way to go,
The lights came on, but ever so low.

Smell of bread and Sunday roast,
Let's check the kitchen and find a ghost.

Witches' brew and hair of dog,
Wing of bird and leg of frog.

Top of the stairs there was a door,
Up in the ceiling there was one more.

Through the door, the girls they crept,
This is where the people slept.

Creaking floorboards and four-poster bed,
Bed bugs running and a deer's head.

The thunder cracked, the lightning flashed,
The lights came on, a mirror smashed.

Top of the stairs, dirt on her head,
'Please, let's go,' Leah said.

Photos, letters and an eight foot bear,
What's that box, over there?

Open the top, let's look inside,
The attic shut, nowhere to hide.

A loud voice said:

'You shouldn't have come and made a mess,
You're stuck forever, goodnight, God bless.'

Lucy Harrison (12)
Lowton High School

JUST ANOTHER FACE IN THE CROWD

I put my face on every day,
It's what you know and love,
Even though it's not the real me.
You wouldn't know the difference,
Because my face is just like everybody else's,
It's not unique in any way.
It's just another face in the crowd.
It does not have its own views,
It just sits in the background, unnoticed.
It never shows its true feelings.
They are hidden deep within.
My face is a good actor,
It's what you expect,
Another soldier following orders.
Maybe it's for the better,
But we will never know,
Because who will ever meet me?
I'm locked away behind the face,
That does not show my true reflection.

But doesn't everyone have a face?

Katie Millward (16)
Lowton High School

Springtime Flare

Springtime is nice,
Springtime is paradise,
Especially for lambs,
With the tossing and turning
Upon the high lands,

Flowers they weave, they whine
And twine,
Sun starts to set,
Round about nine,

The colours they loom,
Like the peacock's plume,
To dazzle and razzle,
Like roses in bloom,

The smell is so lively,
Like freshly cut grass,
The pollen it dances,
To prick and harass.

Suspicious to wonder,
The bees in their flight,
To bob and to hob,
For sailor's delight,

To gaze and to sit,
To stare and to wear,
All for the sake,
Of the springtime flare.

Adele Orrell (13)
Lowton High School

TIGER

I'm creeping through the jungle
following a stripy tiger.
Weaving in and out of the bushes
ducking out the way of spiders.
I've only seen one once before
and that was a wonderful sight.
His fur is glorious and fluffy
and his mind is filled with might.
A tiger is used for so many things
including coats and features.
But the thing I want to stop the most
is the people killing these wonderful creatures.

Danielle Eckersley (13)
Lowton High School

THE SKY

The sky is often littered with clouds,
like random blotches of paint.
I like the sky and its slow movement,
so calm, this sloth of the sky.
Gliding calmly, its great fluffy shapes
slide as they swoosh slowly about the sky.
The sky is never-ending it seems,
stretching along for miles.
In hours the great mass can
totally change its colour.
The gazing it openly invites
is hard to ignore.

Tim Isherwood (13)
Lowton High School

My Friends

Friends mean a lot to me
That's why I have so many
There's Jane and Gemma and Katy
But they are just a few

We natter like old grannies
And have a laugh or two
We look out for each other
That's why we are a crew

We fall out quite a bit
But never really mean it
We make up very quickly
Then that's what good friends do!

Kimberly Bennett (13)
Lowton High School

Gone

My dad's gone,
He went yesterday,
My mum - face like thunder
Tears roll down my cheek
Empty, angry, alone
Why? I ask myself
Why did he have to do it?
Was Mum not good enough?
Do I mean nothing to him?
Questions race through my head
As I try to understand.
It will never be the same.
My dad's gone and he's never coming back.

Lucy Taverner (13)
Lowton High School

White

White is a silent colour,
yet it screams out for company.
White is the missing colour of the rainbow,
hidden but obstructive.
White is the background noise to the noise of the world.

Ever vigilant,
but never at its peak,
white is below average
but superior to all others.

White is the music that is never played,
and the music that was never written.
White is the vengeance that was never wrought,
and never conceived.
White is destructive and all-powerful,
but chooses to shun this power
and live a different life.

Mark Lillas (15)
Lowton High School

My Drums

This is the supreme musical instrument,
Sounding like giants' footsteps.
When dust covers them, it is warning you to use them.
They sit there shining at their audience.
My drums are green, appealing and under my supervision.
At the end of a song I hit the cymbal, it gives a crash!
I am the machine which controls them.
Without drums there would be no such thing as music.
By far they are the most valuable thing to me.

Anthony Shaw (13)
Lowton High School

What Went Wrong?

As I step into this world
It strikes me to see
How greedy and selfish
We all seem to be.

No thought for another
Or the one over there
But if you look different
They'll all stop to stare.

And if you don't fit
The criteria is blunt
You're just an outcast
They're all sure to grunt.

Like jealous old crows
Who just like to steal
They strip them of riches
And of pride and self-esteem.

But yet if we learn
That each life is priceless
And everyone is worth something
Young, bold or lifeless.

Simone Turner (13)
Lowton High School

Smile

A smile is a gift
To treasure and possess.
A symbol of joy and true happiness.

A smile takes nothing,
And gives so much more.
You can smile if you're rich,
You can smile if you're poor.

A smile is like gold,
Precious and true.
When I see a smile it reminds me of you.

A smile is a gift
To treasure and possess.
A symbol of joy and true happiness.

Danielle Wilcock (13)
Lowton High School

Winter Breaks

The warm and secure feelings are leaving,
They've burned out and gone up in smoke,
The once ignited fire has hibernated,
With the strong winds and cold it couldn't cope.

The animals now go down deeper,
With their supplies they snuggle up for the cold,
They can no longer rely on the warm weather,
And now have to rely on resilience.

The green is slowly dying,
The leaves are doomed for a downward spiral,
The once full of life trees in my garden,
Are now more like tall, fragile skeletons.

There's a surprise in the morning as I wake,
There's a blank canvas waiting in my garden,
Waiting for the first footprint of a child,
The enjoyment that will paint it full of vibrant colours.

The days come to an end,
And it is only then that you feel it again,
The warm and secure feeling,
As you lie in your bed and drift off.

Robyn Leigh (15)
Lowton High School

SMOKING KILLS

Why do children smoke?
Because they think they're cool,
But really they just make themselves look a fool,
They think they're big and hard,
But all they do is kill their heart,
And whatever makes them want to start?

So many youngsters smoke,
It's unbelievable why,
As in the end they will only cry,
And think why, oh why!

Mums and dads will have their say,
Whilst other parents give them their own way,
No longer children, but all grown up,
Now is the time it's hard to give up.

Smoking is nasty,
Smoking is cruel,
It causes kids to be fooled,
At the end of the day,
They go their own way.

So what if you get a thrill,
Better start writing your will,
If you don't stop now you're gonna get in deeper,
But one thing's for sure, you're gonna meet the Grim Reaper.

Katy Forshaw (15)
Lowton High School

Whit Walks

You could hear them coming from
streets away, the boom of the drum,
the um-pah of the tuba, and the shrill
toot of the cornet.

The sound gradually swept before
them like flood water coming into
town, silencing the crowd,
dampening their noise.

Then they were in sight, the slanting
rays of the sun shining on them
making each instrument light up
like a torch.

The crowd turned to watch,
gradually the sound filled the air
until it felt that the air must burst
like a too full balloon.

And then all too soon the bright
sounds began to disappear like a train
leaving the station until only the rhythmic
rattling of the wheels was left.

Michael Thomas (14)
Lowton High School

IMPRISONED

Imprisoned,
Trapped in solitude,
The walls of pitiless seclusion
Render my tears,
Wrench my heart.

Incarcerated,
Yearning for the barricade of fear to perish
As I tread the footsteps of despair,
That desire burning inside, brandishing my soul with eternal hatred
For all that behold the essence of happiness.

Desperate,
I long for the membrane of the susceptible trust,
That leads to my vanquish, to acquire strength,
Untangle itself from the web of longing,
Plead for the emptiness to melt from my eyes,
As my urge, my need to encounter love intensifies unbearably.

Finished,
My desperate cries echo off these dungeon walls,
Resentment, adoration coincides, flooding my every thought
Whilst all hope and determination oozes through my extended fingers,
Now only dejection courses through this mindless cage
As I come to realise
There is no escaping this

Imprisonment.

Emma Haworth (15)
Lowton High School

Battle Of The Night

It was slowly turning dusk.
A small set of black eyes
Can be seen squinting through the darkness.
Always on the lookout, always aware,
A look of curiosity.

He sets out and positions himself so he's hidden by the long,
Outstretching arms, scrawny fingers, grabbing
He sees his victims and waits . . .

Seeing his time has come,
He pounces. Fingers grabbing . . .
He is a blur of glowing firelight, a white mountain top.

The hens, dragged from the comfort of their night arcs,
Are left,
The freezing darkness swallows them.
The cockerels exhausted,
Everything a rush, a blur, a mess.

The sun's rays peep over the hilltops,
She gracefully caresses the soft, bloodstained carpet,
The hens no longer asleep in their coops
The geese no longer dream of the morning to come.
The cockerels lost their battle to survive.

And far in the distance the glowing firelight flickers
And is extinguished as it disappears behind a hilltop.

Abi Lomax (15)
Lowton High School

THE HUNT

It waited in the tree,
Huge cumbersome coils
Twisted around thick, sturdy branches.
But the gazelle trod through the undergrowth,
Slowly surveying the tasty plants,
Unaware of the lurking danger.

Zigzags flashed across its back
Illuminated by the shimmering sun,
Forked tongue lashing the air into shapes of death.
But the gazelle sampled the tasty morsels
And delicately drank its worries away,
Unaware of the lurking danger.

Demon eyes lock on flesh,
Piercing and unforgiving,
Glistening with anticipation.
But the gazelle ambled slowly towards the tree
Rejoicing in its dappled shade,
Unaware of the lurking danger.

Down the tree
And through the undergrowth,
Closer, closer, closer . . .
But the gazelle, relaxed and content,
Slowly slipped into a peaceful slumber,
Unaware of the lurking danger.

The snake slithered deftly downwards
As the gazelle turned in its sleep,
Unaware of the lurking danger.
The snake sank in its daggers
And plunged the gazelle into eternal darkness.

Lee Marsden (15)
Lowton High School

THE TIGER

The tiger softly stays behind the grass
Waiting to seduce its prey.
His mouth watering like a tap
Left dripping in the night.

The tiger leaps out from the bull rushes.
His prey, terrified and doesn't dare move.
But now he darts across the fields,
Galloping, running as fast as lightning.

The tiger now darts in the air
Like a firework, he jumps onto the prey
And sticks his teeth into
The flesh and blood, and eats.

Louise Checkley (15)
Lowton High School

THE STORM

The sky was black as night
and full of clouds.
Thunder rumbled,
lightning flashed
and rain pelted the rooftops.
The people outside ran for cover.
The lightning flashed.
The thunder banged one last time.
The rain turned to drizzle.
The clouds separated
and the sun shone through once more.
The storm was over
and I had got through.

James Keefe (12)
Lowton High School

Graveyard

In a snow enshrouded graveyard,
On a hilltop bleak and bare,
Not a single soul is stirring,
No one lingers there.

Until a distant bell tolls midnight,
All spirits are awoken,
They creep and crawl and widely flail,
But still no word is spoken.

They wander round,
Fast and slow,
Floating free and easy,
Hardly daring to greet the glow
Of the sun on a summer evening.

Dawn is creeping gradually,
They lose their peace of mind,
They start to shriek and panic,
And return back underground.

In a snow enshrouded graveyard,
On a hilltop bleak and bare,
Not a single soul is stirring,
No one lingers there.

Catherine Pennington (13)
Lowton High School

Traffic!

Traffic is busy,
Traffic is slow,
It makes you late,
Wherever you go.

Traffic is boring,
Traffic is smelly,
It makes you choke,
Wherever there's smoke.

Jordan Fox (12)
Lowton High School

Day Dreams

The soft summer sun
Sets in the sky
Sending an array of
Mystery and magic
To all that dare see.

The hint of autumn
Just around the corner,
Tempts the cool evening's wind
That sweeps my hair
From my face.

A tinkle of laughter
From far away,
Breaks the hypnotic silence
That has been placed
Upon the world.

As the merging golds and reds
Of the sunset
Melt into the ocean,
Another hazy memory
Of an enchanting summer evening
Comes to a peaceful end.

Katie Piggott (16)
Lowton High School

WHAT AN ENCHANTING PLACE

What an enchanting place,
Strong, vibrant, crashing waves
Erupting against the sculptured coast.
Wild, impressive, dancing waves
Pause momentarily, like holding breath
Then bellow aloud,
Creating a symphony of orchestral harmony.
A silent beauty.
A natural beauty.
Untouched, an unintentional charm.
A Jurassic cliff stands tall, frames unspoilt treasures,
Completes the masterpiece.
A priceless art.
A blink of an eye loses an eternity.
Turn around, cast an eye,
Another work of art.

Close my eyes, skin aglow,
Wind whipping westward,
Restraining movement, competing forces,
Like a tug of war,
Step by step I go.
Senses alive, finely tuned, absorbing the winter sun.
Feeling safe and secure in its beauty.
Snapshot, never gone.

Samantha Coffey (15)
Lowton High School

MONKEY BUSINESS

It can climb like poisonous ivy up a wall,
Swing from tree to tree however tall,
The purpose of it?
To create us - the human
Through the ages we've formed through evolution.

It's not very strong,
There are animals superior to it.
It can escape quicker than you can say . . .
Bananas - the food they love to eat.

It's a clever animal,
It knows how to think,
It's quick at reacting if it's in danger.
It will pounce up through the trees,
Climbing, climbing,
Swinging, swinging.

Louise Henry (15)
Lowton High School

SHE

She is a word,
She is a person.
She is beautiful,
She is kind.
She is made up of something,
Just like us.
She is smooth, silky and sly.
She is fast as a cheetah.
She is crunchy and crispy.
She is a person.

Zoe Sawle (13)
Lowton High School

Winter Is Ace

W inter is cold, winter is white,
I t becomes horrible when you get frostbite,
N ormally it's nice, because we have Christmas,
T ell the truth, so you get visited by Saint Nicholas,
E very day you can play in the snow,
R emembering about the birth of Jesus.

I n winter we get different weathers,
S now, hail and frost are the most common.

A t December it is the coldest,
C old is the word and also freezing,
E njoy the fun of building snowmen, but don't forget
about the abominable snowman.

Kevin Nicholson (12)
Lowton High School

Look At Me

Do you ever look at me?
Do it. Do it now.
Look at me.
What do you see?

Eyes glistening with unshed tears?
Hurt so deep you keep falling?
A look that begs you to listen?
Or do you see what you want to see?

Open your eyes.
You don't care.
But that doesn't mean I don't hurt.

Laura Otty (15)
Lowton High School

SEPTEMBER THE 11TH

I sit
Watching a throat-burning fog
Rise from the graveyard.
As the heroes of red and blue,
Claw at the field of tears,
Almost drowning in the emotion.
I wish I could claw with them,
And find them a speck of hope.

I sit
The haze of the television brings me no warmth.
Only a dull aching numbness,
A swirling black void.
As hate and selfish fears slowly like black tar,
Seep into my cancerous soul.
'Six thousand dead' announces the emotionless newsreader.
But emotionless doesn't exist.

You could've ignored it.
Selfishly turn your unsympathetic back to the torrent of screaming pain
But you know the tormenting torture I'm feeling behind glazed eyes.
Because whatever walls you build to hide it,
Your heart will beat them down.
Will strive to grasp the impact of such pointless devastation.
But imagination has no insight into the souls of destroyed destinies,
Whose hearts have been mercilessly shattered,
Like windows whose fragments now lie among the rubble.

I sit
What else can I do?

Rebecca Grime (15)
Lowton High School

If I Should Be . . .

(Dedicated to my grandad)

If it should be I grow frail and weak
And pain should wake me from my sleep
Then you must do what must be done
For this last battle can't be won.

You will be sad I understand
What is to come will hold no fears
You'll not want me to suffer so
When the time comes please let me go.

I know in time you too will see
That is kindness that you do me
Although my tail its last has waved
From suffering and pain I've been saved

Do not grieve that it should be you
Who has to decide this thing to do
We've been close us two, these years
Don't let your heart hold any tears

Vikki Corbett (13)
Lowton High School

The Secret Love

I think about you every night,
Under the stars shining bright.
But I'll have to wait till day,
To tell you what I must say.

You have to know how I feel,
Because I think this is very real.
I have a secret love for you,
So I know what I must do.

I must be brave, take a chance,
And ask you to the school dance.
You will definitely make my day,
If yes is the word you will say.

I'll tell you what is in my heart,
That we should never be apart.
We'll stay together all the night,
Kissing under the stars so bright.

Chloe Mushrow (12)
Lowton High School

CHRISTMAS TIME

Frost decorating windowpanes
and the spiderwebs whitening.
Icicles hanging from the gutters
wetting passers-by.
Snowmen dressed in adult's clothes
and a little carrot for its nose.
Children's footsteps on the ground, running around
the Christmas tree singing Jingle Bells.
Seeing people laugh and cheer,
meeting their families in the frosty air.
Carol singers loud and clear,
singing merrily for everyone to hear.
Christmas is the time of the year
when everyone is full of cheer.
Little children peacefully sleeping,
while Santa Claus is creeping
carefully into the bedroom
of boys and girls.

Amanda Hutt (12)
Lowton High School

SILENT SERPENT

A mouse amongst solitude, silently awaits,
Yet realising the potential for its constricted fate,
Slithering, slowly, silently together
It gathers its bulk like the wind does a feather.

Unravelled, it slides, extended and intent.
Another meal, but no sign of a needed resent.
The prey is now cornered, infinity surrounds,
The inevitability of transience, abounds

The walls cease; the prey perceives its endangerment.
Infinity ends, the trapped reaches to invent.
The prey screams as the serpent continues to wrap
With impossible escape the serpent's patience snaps.

The heartless beast shows not a glimpse of remorse,
But in order to survive nature has to take its course,
His purpose is not death, more a passion to survive,
Only feared monsters contain insight to stay alive.

Chris Kay (15)
Lowton High School

WINTER!

Short days,
Long nights,
Very cold in the months,
Snow is falling all around,
Icicles are forming above the ground,
Building snowmen is lots of fun,
But it hurts when you fall on your bum,
Winter is slowly coming to an end,
So watch the world make amend.

Christine Ashurst (12)
Lowton High School

BLUEBELLS

Blue like the sky
And I have always wondered why
Bluebells waving in the wind
It must be a lovely thing
To be a bluebell waving in the wind
With no worries and no cares
All the secrets they know
Will always be theirs
Blue like the sky
And I have always wondered why
What secrets they know
And will never show.

Rebecca Lee (13)
Lowton High School

LOVE!

If I go to Heaven
and you're not there,
I'll carve your name
in a golden chair.
If you're not there
by Judgement Day,
I'll know you've gone
The other way.
And just to prove my love is true
I'll give back the angels
Their harps and wings
Just to be with you.

Victoria Cartwright (13)
Lowton High School

Love

Sometimes you're red
Sometimes you're blue
Here's a card
Just for you.
They're so sweet
They're so fine
Just like you
My Valentine!
You kiss me once
You kiss me twice
When I look in your eyes
It's paradise!

Chloe Watts (12)
Lowton High School

The Zebra So Proud

The zebra of the desert
So colourful, so meek
The glory-bound princess
Stood tall

The zebra of such beauty
So confined, so large
While the hunger restricts her
From free onward motion
Depriving her of full action
Causing her such dissatisfaction

The zebras of the world
All packed in close-knit
All huddled together from the hunter
So fit

The zebra of such little land
So blooming full of joy
As they look onwards
Towards the most
Promised land.

Donna Higson (16)
Lowton High School

THE CLOUD'S TEARS

As the happy little cloud
Looks upon our Earth
His tears begin to spread
They spread across our Earth

He has tears all because
He saw our planet so he cried
Because it's in disarray
We cannot calm the cloud's tears
But if we try to save our planet
The little cloud will shine with joy

Then we will have sunshine
For a very long time unless
We turn evil again
But let us hope that
It won't turn out that way.

Kelly Jones (12)
Lowton High School

FEELINGS

Have I done the right thing?
I sometimes dream of what might have been,
Together like a family,
But now I know that could never be.

My sisters and I were once real close,
I broke the bond that day in court,
I don't think that they could ever forgive me,
I made my choice and now I have to live with it.

Like peas in a pod was our family,
We did everything together which was how it should be,
Then came the split which broke all our hearts,
It should never have come to splitting us apart.

I live here, they live there,
Sometimes it's really hard to bear,
I want to scream, shout or maybe cry,
But instead I lock it all up inside.

I ask myself all the time,
Have I done the right thing?
But sometimes I don't want to answer,
For my true feelings can't hide for much longer.

Millicent-Marie Wild (13)
Lowton High School

I Wish My Life Were Simple

I wish my life were simple,
But then what would happen?
No mystery men,
Would peer through my door.

I wish my life were simple,
But then nothing would happen.
No bank robbers
Would charge at the banks I was passing.

I wish my life were simple,
But then my life wouldn't be interesting.
No one
Would bow to my feet.

I wish my life were simple,
But then what would I do?
I would
Have no As in science or English.

I wish my life were simple,
But then what would I do?
What would you do
If your life weren't simple?

Beatrice Lacey (12)
Lowton High School

RABBITS

They are cute and cuddly.
As soft as cotton.
They jump, hop and run around.
They've got big wide eyes and little noses too.
They live in the wild but you can keep them as a pet.
If you keep them in a hutch they will never get wet.
They like to eat grass and carrots too.
They sleep on a bed of straw and get very comfy.
That's why they're so cute and cuddly.

Emma Woodcock (12)
Lowton High School

LOVE

Love is all around us,
And everywhere we go,
The man wears his bow,
The woman wears her dress,
Just to impress.
There are different types of love,
Some are as pure as a dove.
Some is just passion,
Which goes with the fashion.
Everywhere that love is spread,
Sadness is no longer, happiness instead.

Jennifer Lawley (12)
Lowton High School

A Bat

Eyes half open
Eyes half closed
I wish I could see
Further than my nose

Eyes half open
Eyes half closed
Living in a cave
Is where I also doze

Eyes half open
Eyes half closed
My smell is bad
I can't even smell a rose

Eyes half open
Eyes half closed
With my wings wrapped
Round me is a good pose

Eyes half open
Eyes half closed
At the end of my feet
Are quite a few toes.

Charlotte Ashdown (12)
Marple Hall High School

THE BLINDING BARN OWL

His fabulous footsteps were silent,
Cold staring eyes
Glued to his prey,
He is death.

As his blood bearing beak
Rips the once living prey apart,
His waltzing white wings
Are silently soaring back to his lair.

Then he screams a warning,
An eagle owl is descending
Onto his lair,
What shall he do?

His treacherous talons
Suddenly feel weak,
His wings as soft as silk
Suddenly seem stiff,
The family crouches and hides.

The eagle owl ascends,
He is gone,
Now the barn owl can go and hunt again.

His fluffy white feathers
Shine like metal,
As he soars through the
Misty morning sunrise.

Francesca Alimundo (12)
Marple Hall High School

If Only They Knew

When I went into the war,
everyone looked at me with awe.
If only they knew.

The cannonballs have destroyed my ears,
I wish they could destroy my fears.
If only they knew.

My feet have dried up and wrinkled,
my uniform is muddy and crinkled.
If only they knew.

With all the sights I see I wish I was blind,
to think this war is right I must be out of my mind.
If only they knew.

I wish this war was at an end,
so I could be with my family and friends.
If only they knew.

Calum Baglin-Clarke (11)
Marple Hall High School

Autumn

Now it is autumn the leaves will fall down,
Red, yellow, golden brown,
Night will come soon,
Along with the stars and the moon,
It's going to be cold,
I have been told,
Winter is near,
After winter the sky will be clear.

Matthew De Garis (11)
Sale Grammar School

SPACE

Space is beautiful
Space is cool
Space is awesome
Space is no fool

It fills me with wonder
When I gaze into space
Is there life out there?
Is there a human race?

The twinkling little diamonds
Shimmer in the sky
As beautiful as the orbiting Jupiter
As bright as the tiger's eye

Today's the big day
Neil Armstrong flies to space
5, 4, 3, 2, 1, take off!
'The planets seem closer than they are!'

Huge, colourful planets, orbit gracefully through the galaxies
As peaceful as the night sky
The shimmering diamonds slowly fade away
It may be dawn here, but in space there is still a night sky

Space is beautiful
Space is cool
Space is awesome
Space is no fool!

Nina Black (12)
Sale Grammar School

SPACE

Here I am, up in space,
This really is an extraordinary place.
In space there is no light,
To see any humans in our sight.
If we were any closer to the sun,
We would be a hot cross bun.
The ring around Saturn is so fast,
That I'm lucky to see it at last.
Pluto is as cold as ice,
I don't think it'll be very nice.
I want to travel to a star,
But I know it is too far.
There, lurking in the sky,
Hidden in the clouds very high,
I can see a meteoroid,
I wish it would be destroyed.
As far as I assumed,
Our planet would be doomed,
Unless we have enough,
Or some rough stuff.
There are alien forces beyond the moon,
But I didn't expect to see them so soon,
It is a concern,
To look and turn,
To see a UFO in the air,
It will probably make you stare,
And as quick as a fly,
It has vanished in the blink of an eye,
I must now return to land and sea,
After all my planet needs *me!*

Sandeep Rayet (11)
Sale Grammar School

AUTUMN

The autumn has come and the leaves are changing colour,
From green to rich red and gold.
They fall to the ground all crispy and brown.

With the shorter days and the darker nights,
The wind becomes stronger, it whistles and howls.
It already feels colder.

The conkers are growing on the trees,
The squirrels wait for the acorns and nuts to store for the winter.
The hedgehogs now hide under leaves.

The birds are gathering to fly to a warmer place,
It will soon be Hallowe'en and the children trick and treating.
The autumn has come.

Mark Newton (11)
Sale Grammar School

A DIFFERENT VIEW . . . ALMOST A DREAM

In a helicopter,
I look around me, a normal vision,
But then I look out of the window,
And a different view awaits my eyes,
Almost a dream . . .
Cars like a fast-moving current of toys, all different colours,
People like a pattern of coloured dots,
Trees like green lollipops and
Bushes like green splashes of paint,
With sheep like pieces of cotton wool dotted about,
Oh up so high,
In the sky,
Everything is different.

Lewis Jackson (11)
Sale Grammar School

Autumn

The whistling wind shakes the
glistening red leaves off the tree.
The sun is dormant for the season
and is hidden behind the ugly grey clouds.

The squirrels gather their fallen nuts
and bury them so they are sheltered from the weather.
The birds salvage some of the fallen twigs
to add to their nests.

Children appear and grab the conkers
for conker battles at school.
People around seem dismal because of the painful
hailstorms and the destructive winds.

Graham Swift (14)
Sale Grammar School

The Airport

Travellers queuing,
Planes setting off.

Porters like pack horses,
Piling on cases.

Stewards like robots
Directing people to places.

Where are they off to?
Some faraway beaches?

Florida, France, Italy, Spain,
I wish I was going on holiday again!

Richard Agnew (11)
Sale Grammar School

THE CHRISTMAS I GOT NO PRESENTS

The night before Christmas,
I'm really excited,
At what I will get,
Hope I'll be delighted.

As I go up the stairs
To my tidy bedroom,
I'm thinking of Santa
Flying past the moon.

Whilst I am in
My small, warm bed,
I'm having lots of thoughts
In my very tired head.

Music and books?
That jacket I've seen?
Oh, what's the use?
It's better to dream!

When morning came
I was in despair,
My stocking was empty,
There was nothing there!

Mum found me crying
In my favourite chair,
She opened the cupboard,
My presents were there.

I asked her why
She hid them from me,
She said it would teach me
Not to be naughty!

Alexander Wareing (11)
Sale Grammar School

I'VE GOT THE HOOBY-JOOBYS

I've got the hooby-joobys, I've got it everywhere.
I kept it in my wardrobe, but now it's over there!
I'm making it my business to catch it, snatch it.
I really do need it, maybe just a little bit.

I want the hooby-joobys,
But it's always here and there,
One minute it's in the beauty parlour,
The next it's wrestling a bear.

It's like some kind of alien,
It speaks like this:
'A wooby jooby looby!
I've got the smiles!'
But I think it is stupid.

I'm freeing the hooby-joobys,
For they are boring me,
They boiled as I was making
A nice, hot cup of tea.

Now they live on inside me,
Now I've got the smiles,
Now I want to dance,
On my school files.

'What do you want for tea?'
My mum asks,
'A wooby googly toodly!'
I reply, the hooby-joobys have really got inside me.

I'm living on with the hooby-joobys,
And today they still say -
'A wooby jooby looby hooby,'
And there they will stay.

Chris Croston (11)
Sale Grammar School

AUTUMN

Summer goes drifting away,
Autumn comes on its way.
Leaves are falling on the ground,
Crunch, crunch, is their sound.

Red, yellow and green,
These colours can be seen.
Also orange and there is brown,
This coloured carpet covers the ground.

All the trees becoming bare,
Wisps of coldness in the air.
The frost bites at our skin,
And we begin to feel a sting.

The birds will now start their flight,
Together they are a wonderful sight.
Off to the south they will fly,
High above in the deep blue sky.

Coats and hats begin to appear,
Scarves and muffs warm up the ear.
But winter is creeping up behind,
Soon autumn will be thrown aside.

Caroline Parker (11)
Sale Grammar School

FROM UP ABOVE

From up above
The people as miniature as ants
Scurrying about.

From up above
Little toys can go by
Driving from place to place.

From up above
Houses like models
Millions of them cramped up in tiny spaces.

From up above
Forests like small garden weeds
And bird-like flies inside.

Gary Voss (11)
Sale Grammar School

FIRST DAY AT SCHOOL

As my mum always said,
'Going to secondary school is a big step.'
As I found out today.
Getting crushed into the wall,
From the biggest to the small.
That lunch queue's so long,
When I arrive, the chips are gone!
Trying to find my way to classrooms,
One lesson's in three different places,
It's exhausting!
Four times as big as my old school,
Four times the length to get there,
The place is a maze!
Different kit for PE,
Remember your protractor for maths,
Don't forget your name card in English,
Or your folder for science.
So at the end of the week,
I'm really quite shattered, wouldn't you think?

Mark Andrews (11)
Sale Grammar School

My Pet

His soft golden fur was huddled upstairs,
His whiskers would twitch to and fro,
His small little body would sleep all day long,
For his presence you'd never know.

From his dark little den into sunlight he'd come,
He would struggle and squirm to get free,
His thin little body could squeeze through anything,
But he'd never escape from me.

But as he got older he would drag his back legs,
And most of the time sit still,
His appetite waned and no weight did he gain,
As he got very seriously ill.

Then as time slowed down and suddenly stood still,
A lump appeared in my throat,
For the day had come when he must leave us all,
On a sad but memorable note.

Jessica Boardman (11)
Sale Grammar School

Space

As I gazed into the sky above
I instantly fell in love
With the many stars in the sky
That drift far and float so high.

David Bajela (12)
Sale Grammar School

MOBILE PHONES

Someone's got a message,
We all check our phones,
Is it me or is it him?
We all have different tones.

The message is for me, hooray,
I wonder who it's from,
Is it Jack or is it Phil,
Or maybe Nick or Tom?

Our phones have different covers,
And lots of games to play,
My mum says I will waste the battery,
When I play them all day.

I have to check my credit,
By dialling 5-4-3.
The evil voice at the other end
Says I only have 6p.

It's not enough to text my mum
And tell her I'll be late,
So I'll be in big trouble
When she meets me at the gate.

Everywhere you go these days,
The world is full of phones,
In churches, libraries, schools and parks,
You can't avoid the tones!

Simon Stewart (11)
Sale Grammar School

THE THING I MET IN THE WOODS ONE DAY

I met it in the woods one day
It had big, hairy, purple feet
And claws the size of my dad!

I met it in the woods one day
It had short, stumpy, orange legs
And knees the size of horses

I met it in the woods one day
It had a big, fat, green belly
With a tiny T-shirt with 'flobbajack' on it

I met it in the woods one day
It had long, scary, hairy arms
And fingers as long as me

I met it in the woods one day
It had a head the size of a thousand footballs
And jaws with teeth of steel

'Go away! Go away!'
He screamed and jumped,
'I'm the flobbajack. Run! Run!'

Callum Tew (11)
Sale Grammar School

SCRAPING THE SKY

Towering over the world,
Scraping the sky,
Glaring down at the city,
Wondering why,
All the people,
The cars and the plants,
Are centimetres high,
And look like ants!

Towering over the world,
Looking down,
On the matchstick people,
In the toy town,
As the fairy lights illuminate the street,
I silently stand,
Watching old friends meet.

Hollie Craven (11)
Sale Grammar School

All Year Round

You can never tell
What the weather's going to be like.
Rain, snow, sunshine
Or windy weather to fly my kite.

Even the weathermen don't know
What the weather's going to be like tomorrow.
Winter is the best season I know
Because of the clean, white snow.

I like spring very much
Because of the beautiful flowers and their smooth touch.
I like summer quite a lot
With all the pretty forget-me-nots.

I like autumn ever so much
Because October is my birthday month.

Each day is unique,
Each day is a surprise,
Each day is different from the next,
Each day has a beautiful sunrise.

Jessica Price (12)
Sale Grammar School

I Dream

I dream I am a butterfly, flying through the sky
I dream I am a rabbit, to watch the day go by
I dream I am a cat, all furry and fluffy
I dream I am a dog, a right tough tutty!

I dream I am an adult, no school!
I dream I am a pop star, oh how cool!
I dream I am an actor, on ITV
I dream I am an air hostess, what a lot to see!

I dream I am a house, all warm and snug
I dream I am a church, 1000 times as big as a bug!
I dream I am an office, 10 storeys high
I dream I am a college, how hard they all try!

I dream I am a light, glowing so bright
I dream I am a couch, as long as the weight is light!
I dream I am a picture, showing off some art
I dream I am a table, but that would be a lark!

Victoria Leather (11)
Sale Grammar School

Autumn Wind

The wind races through the street,
As fast as an express train.
It thrusts through the sky,
Like a turbo boosted jet plane.
The trees part with the leaves,
Which float to the ground.
It swirls them back up again,
Like a merry-go-round.

Adam George (11)
Sale Grammar School

How Not To Wash A Cat

My cat's a mess
She's got mud on my dress
And I've never seen a moggy
That was so soggy
Her whiskers are crumpled
Her fur is matted
So to make her posher
I'll have to wash her
Down with the mat
In with the cat
Spotting a mouse
She ran out of the house
On no, that's bad luck
She's gone back in the muck.

Sophie Robinson (11)
Sale Grammar School

School!

School, school, it's a drag,
All the teachers do is nag,
I wake too early.

We never have fun,
Only brilliant high marks,
In our best daydreams.

After school is cool,
All you do is play and rest,
But hang on - homework!

Alisha Patel (11)
Sale Grammar School

TESTS

Some tests are hard, some tests are easy,
Some just say they are too easy peasy.
Most tests make me vibrate with shivers,
Right up to my pumping liver.
I put my pen on the paper,
And I feel like I am in pain.
When I stare at the questions,
I feel I am going insane.
My brain is going one way and my eyes are going the other,
This is the time when I really need my mother.
My brain wants to scream,
But all I want to do is let off some steam.
Oh, oh do I look pale?
I'm really scared if I'm going to fail.
And here I am twisting my hair, thinking about my looks,
Oh forget that, let's hit straight to the books.
Oh thank goodness, the test is over,
It was really *easy*, honest!

Maria Vassiliou (11)
Sale Grammar School

THE ALIENS HAVE LANDED

The aliens have landed
They're in our back garden right now
I invited all my friends
And they all said, 'Wow'

How amazing, how fantastic
But they seem to look like plastic
They're not, really they're not
They're real, not plastic, nor pot

At night they move and they walk
They sing and they talk
They're all slimy and like jellies
And they wear big red wellies

They're going tomorrow
In their big giant teapot
I wish they weren't going
I wish they were *not!*

Sarah Butler (11)
Sale Grammar School

MY CAT

My cat Jess is black and white
She has big green eyes that stare at you
She has white paws and whiskers like an otter
Jess is very big even though she's two

Sometimes Jess thinks she's a dog
As she likes to play fetch and chase balls
She plays with rope and chases her tail
She brings presents - mice, birds and all

At mealtimes she begs for her food
She miaows when she wants something
She purrs loudly when she gets it
Especially when she hears the microwave ting

Jess is a very independent cat
But she sometimes sits on your knee
She gets very angry when I tease her
And ends up scratching me.

Melissa Monteiro (12)
Sale Grammar School

THE CAT

Cat, cat, catching a mouse
Please don't give it to Mum now
And keep it out of the house

Cat, cat, sneak through the leaves
With a wiggle of your body
And jump in the breeze

Cat, cat, you naughty little kitten
Don't scratch at all the furniture
Or you'll end up in a mitten

Cat, cat, in the night
Your eyes are glowing
Shiny and bright

Cat, cat, my sweet little friend
You listen quite intently
All my worries you mend

Cat, cat, sat by the fire
Curled up on the mat
As long as you desire

Cat, cat, with a purr and miaow
Sit comfy on my lap
And let me stroke you now.

Meloney Flanagan (11)
Sale Grammar School

DOWN FROM A PLANE

On a plane if you look down
You'll see the houses small and brown
The people are like ants scurrying around
The cars like bugs crossing the ground

The clouds are fluffy like cotton wool
The forest you see is very full
The river curves like a winding snake
And if you look closely you'll see a lake.

Mark Heighway (11)
Sale Grammar School

CITY

As I enter the ground,
I hit the loud sound,
It's all blue,
There is no dew,
The away and the home fans are apart,
The match is about to start,
3-2-1!

City's got the ball,
But now the defenders have got it all,
The away fans are a bore,
Oh yes, what is the score?
The City fans are singing a ditty,
It's 3-0 to City!

The final whistle blows,
But not everyone goes,
The City crowd
Is very loud,
Now the noise is dying,
The away fans are still crying,
But now it's time to go away,
We'll be back another day.

Elizabeth Carlton (11)
Sale Grammar School

THE WEREWOLF

Be wary of the werewolf wild,
He's very big and hairy,
His favourite meal's a little child,
His favourite mode is scary.

His claws are black and sharp and long,
His eyes are gruesome red,
His teeth are yellow, sharp and strong,
He howls when we're in bed.

At dead of night he starts to creep,
And prowl in pale moonlight,
Is there a child not yet asleep?
He's feeling like a bite.

So go to bed and go to sleep,
As soon as you are able,
Or you will be in trouble deep,
In a dish on a werewolf's table.

Piers Halley (12)
Sale Grammar School

ALL THE POWER OF HAYSTACKS

The roads curl like wiggly worms,
Fields like a huge green cloth,
Covering the land.
Houses like lifeless ants,
Lying in the sun.
And the river curls across,
Like water on a cloth.
But no people do you see.

Sarah Bagshaw (11)
Sale Grammar School

NIGHT

Night is cold and lonely,
With droopy translucent eyes.
Its hair is long and wavy,
And its clothes are very aged.

When the moon shines,
Night will sneak out of its cave,
And go into the country,
Big cities and towns.

It will go into your home,
And slide through your front door,
And into your room,
Where it will turn your bad dreams into good.

When its job has been done,
It will slide back out of your door,
And back to its cave where it shall rest,
Until the moon comes out again.

Georgina Blackburn (11)
Sale Grammar School

LOOKING DOWN

Fields like icing on a cake
With little cotton wool balls,
Sheep!
Cars scuttling like beetles,
Along a never-ending grey snake,
The road!
Wind whistling like the postman,
Bearing no tune.

Clare Crookall (11)
Sale Grammar School

The Bin

A bin is a locust,
Gobbling everything up,
It shovels up food,
But never uses the loo,
It's never full up,
My mum just swaps its stomach and puts it away on the drive,
It tackles every obstacle,
By sucking up everything like a vacuum,
It never moves,
It does not hunt,
It does like buns,
It just gets fed by someone,
Someone tall,
Someone mysterious,
Someone who is an adult . . .
My mum!

Michael Stewart (11)
Sale Grammar School

The Rubbish Truck

Once a week, or sometimes twice
A horrible creature that's not very nice
Comes down our street and we offer it food
As it burps and grunts loudly and acts really crude
With its human slaves working by its side
They move it off with an uneasy slide
Its large meal complete, it ends its day
And rolls itself backwards, moving away.

Daniel Norton (11)
Sale Grammar School

ENGLAND V GREECE

'Twas on a sunny Saturday
October the 6th
Is the date the match lay
The final team had been picked

Old Trafford the place
What a huge crowd
World Cup the race
They all shouted loud

The teams they lined up
The anthems were sung
Qualify for the cup or
Sven Gor will be hung

Then the match began
Nobody was sure
The players they ran
Greece just had to score

Then on came a saviour
His name was Ted
He did it for us
He used his head

Just when we thought
England would get through
The defence they were caught
Greece made it two

The nation couldn't believe it
Was it skill or good luck
A last minute free kick
Reserves our place in the cup.

Matthew Clough (12)
Sale Grammar School

THE NIGHT

The black sky,
a silk, violet sheet,
spread over the sun,
sprinkles of glitter,
glow like bright stars.

The black sky,
a silk violet sheet,
the white light,
of the emulsion moon,
reflecting on calm lakes.

The black sky,
a silk violet sheet,
the sparkling planets,
the spinning ring of Saturn,
the blue cold of Pluto.

The black sky,
a silk violet sheet,
shooting stars,
blasting fireworks,
spinning wheels of laughter.

Thomas Hurford (13)
Sale Grammar School

LOOKING DOWN

Slopes like endless vertical slides,
Rocks sliding down like a child,
Lava like a bowl of tomato soup,
Small stones like Rice Krispies.

No sign of life at all,
Miles of landscape,
Like a quilt spread over the ground,
No sound, there's no sound.

Abigail Oliver (11)
Sale Grammar School

Hunger

I went round to my friend's house one day,
She'd been to the pet store,
Bought two goldfish in a tank,
But she wanted something more.

The next day I went to my friend's house,
She had got a can now,
She liked its furry whiskers,
But she wanted a brown cow.

The next day I met her on the farm,
She'd got the cow of course,
The told me what she wanted,
She'd always wanted a horse.

The next day we met at the racecourse,
With horse and dog too,
She told me what she wanted,
She wanted a zoo!

I met her at the zoo on Friday,
A cup of milk I saw,
A lion, an open cage,
And my friend wasn't there anymore.

Kelsey Marshall (11)
Sale Grammar School

FOOTBALL

What's the point of kicking a ball?
It doesn't matter if you're small or tall,
All the cups, trophies and shields,
And why play on big fields?

He tackles, he passes, he shoots, he scores!
A dog could do that using its paws.
It is quite fun you have to admit,
And I do rate it quite a bit.

Some people say, 'Footballers are thick!'
But at least they can kick.
And some people say, 'What a game!'
The other say, 'They're all the same!'

All the teams that people support,
If they want to play like their heroes they have to be taught,
It can be hard, all that training to attack and defend,
But it's worth it in the end.

Laura Watmough (11)
Sale Grammar School

PIANO - OR SHOULD I SAY SONGBIRD

A songbird tunefully singing,
Black and white feathers pressed down by the wind,
All grouped together, rhythmically playing,
Never making a single mistake,
Once the bird stops, no more playing,
Until it starts flying once again.

Jennifer Evans (12)
Sale Grammar School

NIGHT

Night is a person dark and cold,
He sits on a mountain waiting for the time when
He spreads his long cloak across the highest peak.

He stands,
Tall like a giant, straight as a wall.
Now the time has come.
He runs faster than the gushing wind that lets
The long black cloak touch the ceiling of that sky.

Suddenly it became night and he reached out
Of his pockets, he splashed the stars all over the sullen sky.
Then the brightest ball you've ever seen floats onto its spot.

Finally the lonely man has done his job and
Must now sleep on the same dull mountain
Where no man can find him.

Atina Konarki (12)
Sale Grammar School

ALL NIGHT LONG

The noise of a car
Is an innocent person choking on smoke,
All night long.

The whiteness of the glistening car,
Is as white as a gentle dove,
All night long.

The sight of the beautiful car,
Is as dawning sunset in glistening gold,
All night long.

Rebecca Hedemalm (11)
Sale Grammar School

My Friend's Family

Her mother's lazy
And sleeps most days.
Even though she cleans and pays
For all the clothes you could want,
She's still the best mum you could get.

Her father's tall, big and great,
For all the things he lets you do.
He's into gadgets, computers and footie,
He plays his heavy metal music, so loud,
And wears his gruesome T-shirts in and around.

Her brother is absolutely naughty!
Always hurting his father and sister,
Although he's soft inside.
He plays with dinosaurs,
And watches Scooby Doo!

Charlotte Bleackley (12)
Sale Grammar School

My Mountain View

From the mountain peak,
I see,
Snow coated evenly.
A white blanket spread over the ground,
Falling softly, it doesn't make a sound.
Trees like scarecrows huddled in a bunch,
Each step I take, brings a crunch.
The stream as clear as a pane of glass,
Fish frozen in time, not able to pass.
This is what I see,
From the mountain peak.

Catherine Bell (11)
Sale Grammar School

Rabbit

Little rabbit, young and sweet,
It has brown fur and little feet,
Long, floppy ears, a fluffy white tail,
A pink button nose and a cute smile.

This little bunny seeks attention,
Always loves to be stroked,
Whenever she's tired she will curl up in a ball,
Then sleep till she doesn't want to sleep anymore.

She loves to run round in the garden,
Eat the grass as well,
Sometimes she will roll around in the sun,
Or other times she'll just have no fun.

Catherine Ainsworth (12)
Sale Grammar School

Looking Down

Looking down from the mountain tops,
I see things like I've never seen them before.
The rivers and roads like worms and snakes,
Squirming and curving around and around.
The trees are more like clusters of grass,
Blowing in the breeze.
Looking down from the mountain tops,
The houses and buildings are like tiny pebbles,
Brown in colour and in big long lines.
Looking down from the mountain tops.

Alex Hall (11)
Sale Grammar School

My Pencil Case

A pencil never stops all day,
It writes to the end all the way.
It never shouts back or says,
'I'm tired, put me down; I've worked all day!'

A ruler is on the straight and narrow,
It never curves or bends.
It is like a motorway,
That never ends.

A rubber is a funny thing,
You can write down anything.
It will vanish it like magic.

Felt tips come in many colours,
They bring a rainbow to my paper.
Green, blue, yellow and pink,
They're so bright they make me blink!

Elizabeth Butler (11)
Sale Grammar School

The Car

The car bumped down the road
It swerved
It squeaked
And people peeped
Its eyes lit up
And it sang hup-hup
With skin of steel
And rubber heel
The car bumped down the road.

Christopher Nelson (11)
Sale Grammar School

FRIENDS

I walked in, they looked and laughed.
What had I done? I wanted to know.
Was it my fault? Yes or no?

I thought they were my friends.
I obviously thought wrong.
Picking on me, would this day carry on?

They continued talking.
I knew it was about me.
Staring and pointing, they were as happy as could be.

Their eyes were like eagles'
Spotting their next prey,
What should I do? What should I say?

Rebecca Handy (12)
Sale Grammar School

THE PLAYSTATION MAN

The disc spinning is his heart beating
That humming is his pulse
The lens is his eye
Graphics are his brain sending messages
Directional buttons are his sense of direction
Actions buttons make him move and stop
Each piece of software is more to learn
Each game is a different mood
Each bleep, another tantrum
This is my PlayStation man.

Joe Hindle (12)
Sale Grammar School

WATERFALL!

As tranquil as a sleeping child
Floating in a dream
Glittering brightly in the blinding sun
A gently rippling stream.

Weaving, dodging jagged rocks
Bubbling on its way
Meandering, curving through its course
Its shining hair on display.

Rushing water appears ahead
Gushing with tremendous power
Tearing anything in its path
Looking for anything it can devour.

Running into the jaws of hell
A thundering stampede
Erupting like a furious volcano
Hurtling down with speed.

Rachael Philip (11)
Sale Grammar School

TORMENTED

Lost in a sea of darkness,
Surrounded by hate,
Spinning round and round,
Is this my fate?
Watching and waiting,
Crying and hating,
I am tormented.

Emma Sharples (12)
Sale Grammar School

A Special Moment

'All get together now,' said John,
'Huddle up and make sure you all get on.'
'Billy, stop messing, we haven't got time!'
'Yes, Auntie Shelly, your hair looks fine.'

'Andy, will you put your beer down,
We don't want people thinking we're from rough end of town!'
'Now is everyone ready, Martin put your cig out,
And little Sophie Marie do you want a clout?'

'At the front we want the bride and groom,
And make sure the bridesmaids have plenty of room.'
'Now dads get together with mums by your side,
Everyone else stand around the outside.'

'Now everybody, if you please,
When I give a nod, I want you to say cheese!'
Click went the camera, a moment was made,
Pictures will last, where memories may fade.

Francheska Dowling (12)
Sale Grammar School

Sweets

S ugary sweets, sour sweets, all different kinds of sweets,
W hen you buy the sweets it makes your mouth water
thinking of them,
E ating them is the best thing to do so don't save them! Eat them!
E ach time you buy a sweet money is thrown away.
T angy sweets, tasty sweets, all different kinds of sweets,
S o what is your favourite sweet?

Alexandra Packman (11)
Sale Grammar School

THE SEASONS

The trees are blowing
In the speeding wind
The birds are singing
In the cool breeze
The wind is swishing
As fast as it can
And the leaves are falling
Swirling round and round.

The ground is grey and wet
In the falling rain
The air is freezing
In the rocky hail
The floor is slippy
On the frosty ground
But we are drippy and wet
For a time once again.

The sky is bright and yellow
In the beating sun
The clouds are dull
In the coolness of winter
The sky is pitch-black
In the eerie night
But we are fast asleep
In our warm and cosy beds.

Kieran McDowell (11)
Sale Grammar School

THE SEASONS

Spring, summer, autumn, winter.
Round and round the seasons go.

Yellow, white and orange daffodils
Appear as if by magic.
Buds sprout,
Lambs are born
And animals awake from hibernation.

The bright, powerful sun
Shines his rays down on us.
Animals work merrily,
The trees are green
And we enjoy the holidays.

The leaves change to
Red, brown and orange.
Conkers fall and break,
The weather turns cold
And puddles are everywhere.

The sky turns grey
With rain and mist.
The trees are bare and lifeless,
Animals are in hibernation
And we play in the brilliant, white snow.

Spring, summer, autumn, winter.
Round and round the seasons go.

Suzy Whatmough (12)
Sale Grammar School

My Swimming Challenge

It was my first ever swimming badge,
I was quite excited but nervous, in fact
And thought that I'd do well
Even if I didn't pass
It was only just a bit of fun
So why if I didn't pass, should I feel glum?

It was my turn next
The water looked so deep
My heart started pounding
As the teacher called my name
And as I slid carefully in
I was thinking
Even if I didn't pass
It is just a bit of fun
So why if I didn't pass, should I feel glum?

There I go!
Gliding free
I look back
Everyone's smiling at me
I feel great
The water isn't that deep
It is quite warm, you'll see
Even if I didn't pass
It is just a bit of fun
So why if I didn't pass, should I feel glum?

Yes, yes, I've finished the course
I climb out, cold as ice, shivering, shaking like a bowl of jelly
I stroll to the teacher who doesn't look very nice
'Here you go, well done, well done,' she says in a sweet sort of voice
Even if I didn't pass
It is just a bit of fun
So why if I didn't pass, should I feel glum?

Alexandra Birkmire (11)
Sale Grammar School

SCHOOL

I have just started a new school
And I think it's rather cool
Like the rest I'm dressed in black
Looking for a place at the back

It's the start of a brand new year
I can't believe I'm really here
Difficult to find my way round
My feet hardly touch the ground

We are going on a trip
I have to hand in a slip
We're going to Boreatton Park
Where we'll play until it's really dark

Locker keys have arrived at last
Every day disappears so fast
Head in a spin, I want to scream
Perhaps it's all only a dream?

Laura Barrett (11)
Sale Grammar School

Martin The Warrior

(From 'Tales Of Redwall')

There once was a very brave mouse,
and Martin was his name.
He lived in the woods - not a house -
and wasn't very tame.

This mouse was no ordinary one,
he was a fighter.
The slaves all woke up to find him gone,
when the day was brighter.

Bladrang, the slave master,
found a small hole.
So Martin had to dig much faster,
alongside Grumm the mole.

Grumm the mole and a mouse called Rose,
helped Martin on his way.
They got attacked by lots of crows,
and had no time to play.

Now Martin is locked away,
in a distant cell.
Hoping he'll get out today,
and not stay in hell.

Heather Reynolds (11)
Sale Grammar School

A Bird's Life Beginning To . . . End

Trapped in a shell, you battle,
Kicking, pushing, stretching,
You're free at last from your eggy prison.

As you grow Mother pushes you from the nest,
The newborn chicks must take their first flight;
But will hopefully stay airborne.

'Spread your wings, feel the wonders of flight,
Flap your wings, float, take flight,
Take flight like a kite in the wind.'

They flap and they flap,
They stay in the tree,
Three sad little chicks go back to their mother's lap,
They sob into the mother's feathery knee.

You try and you try until you have success,
Then you find someone to caress,
Someone to care for , someone to be there for.

Now your life has flown by, you have chicks of your own,
It is time to go; though your family grieve,
You make one last request,
'No one must use this nest'
Too late now, you've gone to watch over,
With love and interest.

Kathryn Briggs (11)
Sale Grammar School

I Dreamed Last Night . . .

I dreamed last night I was an angel,
with great big wings to fly anywhere.

I dreamed last night I was a bug,
so small, so small you could not see.

I dreamed last night I was in Heaven,
big gold gates and long gold streets.

I dreamed last night I was a teacher,
1, 2, 3, A, B, C.

I dreamed last night I was me,
all snug and warm asleep, that is how I like to be.

Jordan Cox-Rogers (11)
Sale Grammar School

Tiddles

A little ginger ball of fur,
A tiny, pink, wet nose,
If you listen hard you'll hear his purr,
He's happy I suppose!
Mischief gleaming in his eyes,
It's always time for play,
Full of fun and cute surprise,
Every day's a happy day,
When at last it's time for bed,
As day comes to an end,
It's time to rest your kitten head,
My little sleepy friend.

Christopher Capon (11)
Sale Grammar School

THE LIGHT OF MYSTERY

A dark room,
No shadows to be seen.
An open window,
A cool summer's breeze,
Whistling, whistling.

Clouds in the sky,
Drifting gracefully by,
Queuing in a line,
Only to reveal a face,
Shining, shining.

A beam shimmering,
To reveal a room,
Drowning every item in light,
Shadows come alive,
Dancing, dancing.

No corner,
Can escape the sparkle,
Suffocating in the brightness,
It sits in space,
Watching, watching.

A few hours every night,
This mysterious light appears,
Then leaves,
Stealing shadows,
And lets the world dream . . .

Kirsty Leigh (12)
Sale Grammar School

THE SEASONS

Autumn is here,
The leaves are falling down,
Orange and red,
Yellow and brown,
The temperature drops,
But not too low,
The weather gets colder,
Ready for the snow.

Now it's wintertime,
The ground is very hard,
Ice makes it slippery,
Best be on your guard.
Now it's started snowing,
Wrap up nice and warm,
The snow is very deep,
Build a snowman on the lawn.

Spring has come,
The leaves have grown again,
Helped by a lot
Of sun and heavy rain.
Lots of little animals,
Are being born,
Lambs and chicks,
And a baby fawn.

At last it is summer,
No more school,
Playing on the beach,
Lounging round the pool.
The temperature is rising,
The sun is really hot,
Don't forget your suncream,
Or you will burn a lot.

Jessica Green (11)
Sale Grammar School

The Universe

The universe is a black, speckled sea,
With wave upon wave of galaxies,
Spinning with stars bunched like foam,
Each with its own worlds,
Orbiting great balls of fire.

The universe is the dark depth
Of the ocean floor holding
Undiscovered surprises at every turn,
Unknown planets and beasts of rock destroying
Life, with their first blow.

The universe is an eternity of mystery,
No one knowing whether it ends,
If life exists on different worlds,
If there are other worlds,
Something man is not meant to know.

Jonathan Dunn (12)
Sale Grammar School

FLOWERS

Flowers in my garden,
Flowers in the sun,
Children making daisy chains,
Children having fun.

Delicate little petals,
With a bright green leaf,
Carefully interwoven,
Like a Christmas wreath.

Bright red roses,
With a nasty thorn,
Little closed buds,
Waiting to be born.

The scent is surrounding me,
Going to my head,
Lovely colours everywhere,
In my flower bed.

Giant sunflower head,
Standing strong and tall,
Watching over the daisies,
So petite and small.

Laura Burgoine (11)
Sale Grammar School

MEMORIES

A terrapin
A damp brown and red
Gleaming eyes
And leaf-green head
Lazy and slimy, looked quite bored
Once was abandoned, now is adored

Hale Bop over Corfe Castle
The glowing comet glides high
Up in space
It soars so high
Tail of fire, head of ice
The picture I saw seemed full of life.

Ben Mitchell (11)
Sale Grammar School

Seasons

The spring is coming
The animals come out
The green grass is growing
And the daffodils spout

The summer is coming
The children come out
They have jelly and ice cream
And swim all about

The autumn is coming
The leaves all come down
Animals go to hibernate
Empty trees all around

The winter is coming
The white snow falls
No animals can be seen
And children throw snowballs

The spring is coming
The animals are about
The green grass is growing
A new year has come out.

Philip Richardson (12)
Sale Grammar School

SEASONS

When the winter comes the sun dies away,
But the coldness rises through each day,
The rain crashes down like lightning bolts,
But the calm, soft snow trickles down like salt.

When the spring comes, everything becomes alive,
Even the bees coming buzzing out of hives,
The plants start to grow,
Through the dreaded snow,
And the sun comes out again when spring begins to go.

When summer comes, the sun comes out,
And its glorious light spreads about,
It warms up every place,
Which shines with the light from its face.

The leaves turn brown when autumn arrives,
And becomes dead instead of alive,
They fall from the tree,
And drop a seed as small as a pea.

They wait again, once more,
For winter to come and the rain to pour.

Georgina Charnock (11)
Sale Grammar School

WINTER SNOWFLAKES

Snowflakes dancing in the air,
Twisting and turning so debonair.
Floating in their waltz above,
They come to land,
Softly in the palm of my hand.

Jonathon Morris (13)
Sale Grammar School

The Flower Bud

Little bud, little bud,
What will you be?
Growing on the little bush,
For all folk to see.

I gave you lots of water,
I also gave you sunlight.
I gave you plant food and soil,
Will you grow in the night?

As I was sleeping,
In my warm, cosy bed,
My little bud grew,
Into a small rose of red!

Little rose, little rose,
You are my favourite flower.
Thanks to you, my little red rose,
My garden has flower power.

Nathan Everett (11)
Sale Grammar School

Teachers

T eaching their lessons very happily
E asily marking all the homework
A bsolutely crazy species
C hecking their pupils' answers in class time
H elpful advice if we are stuck
E ducation being taught with pleasure
R eading, writing and listening being taught
S houting at all the naughty students.

Christian Guy (12)
Sale Grammar School

Feel The Vibe

'Music is my first love',
as the old song goes,
from hip-hop to teen-pop
moving on up to soul.

Whether it's disco, bee-bop, cool-pop or jazz,
people everywhere just want to dance!

Music is an inspiration,
it can make you laugh or cry.
It carries special memories
until the day we die.

As individual as oneself
the melodies remain,
no matter where you hear them
you will always feel the same.

So gather up your music,
come and feel the vibe.
It's good to be together,
and have a funky time.

Gemma Williams (12)
Sale Grammar School

Under My Bed

One night I heard a noise,
I heard something moving about,
I looked underneath to see what was there,
And began to scream and shout.

'There's something there,' I shouted.
My mum came in,
Stumbled over the mat
To find . . . the cat.

The poor cat was covered in fluff,
All grey instead of brown.
My mum looked at me with a frown,
And said, 'Get rid of that cat!'

Victoria Castle (12)
Sale Grammar School

FIGHTER NUMBER 1111: MY FATHER

You went to war,
You went to fight,
You went to battle,
You fought at night.

Given a plane,
You flew it high,
You flew it free,
You touched the sky.

You flew happy,
You flew sad,
You thought of me,
I thought of my dad.

You met a Nazi,
You met your fate,
You shot your guns,
You were too late.

We received the telegram,
We sent you to Heaven,
We'll see you there,
Fighter one, one, eleven.

Helen Laybourn (12)
Sale Grammar School

BUZZY BEE

Buzzy Bee flying high
Buzzy Bee in the sky
Buzzy Bee fell to the ground
Ants carried him underground

Buzzy Bee tried to run
Cos he had a little son
Buzzy Bee went and flew
But got caught in sticky goo

Buzzy Bee got stuck
In the rather smelly muck
He then had the idea to eat
The muck, after hours came out his feet

And off he flew into the night
After a day of fear and fright
Back to his home
Under a very pretty gnome.

Geoffrey Smith (12)
Sale Grammar School

THE WAVE RIDER

A boat floats swiftly on the sea,
Oh how I wish that it was me.
The front goes up, the back goes down,
As it starts bobbing around and around.

The sails go up to trap the wind,
As it sails on the sea.
When the wind starts to die down,
The sails fall to the ground.

I watch the boat drift further and further,
As it rides out to sea.
I can just see it on the horizon,
As small as can be.

James Harrison (11)
Sale Grammar School

LONELY

As he sits all alone in his corner,
The corner well known all around the playground,
No one goes there except him,
No one notices the lonely boy in the corner!

He's there every break,
And every break he stays alone,
People just ignore him, like he's not there,
No one notices the lonely boy in the corner!

Never invited into games,
Never brings attention to himself,
Never had a friend,
No one notices the lonely boy in the corner!

Sometimes he wishes he could be more like them,
Just to fit in for one time in his life,
But it never happens,
No one notices the lonely boy in the corner!

Children playing games,
Laughing, shouting, then silence as the bell goes,
Eventually the playground is empty,
And the lonely corner is left lonely!

Lisa Thorpe (12)
Sale Grammar School

Evil Neighbours

If you ever get the chance to meet
That weird family across our street,
I suggest you turn, before it's too late,
And make a swift and speedy escape!

The woman of the house looks like a witch,
With a very noticeable nervous twitch.
How old is she? Who can tell?
She looks like something that rose from Hell.
And if you ever see her unkempt hair,
Watch out, we're sure there are spiders lurking in there.

The husband is quite arguably
The grumpiest man you will ever see.
On the regular occasions my ball goes up his tree,
He mutters and tutters and swears at me.
I can honestly say they're a perfect pair,
Him with his swearing and her with her hair.

Daniel Allcock (12)
Sale Grammar School

Rainforest

Aliens crash-land in the rainforest.
Rain pouring from grey clouds and a blow of
Smoke as the Indians' campfire goes out.
Crickets hurrying around the rotten logs,
Terrified of the storm.
A shine of bright light through the cloud,
Then animals peep through holes.
As the rainforest comes back to life.

Richard Slater (12)
Sale Grammar School

The Rain

Staring out my misty window
Looking out onto the rain
Pitter-patter on the roof
Thinking of what to do.

Watching as it rains so hard
Splishing, splashing on the roof
Seeing children having fun
Looking out my bedroom window.

Looking out onto the sky
Seeing rainbows up so high
Looking up the sun comes out
Happy as I can go out.

James Williams (12)
Sale Grammar School

The Guessing Game

I am: A stealth assassin,
A silent sleeper,
A little cushion,
A superb creeper,
A fluffy ball,
A great leaper,
A fearful killer,
A body of knives,
I have nine lives,
A wild thing,
A home thing.

I am a cat.

Daniel Sweetman (11)
Sale Grammar School

TIGER

Black
Gold
Fur
Bold

Whiskers
Ear
Eyes
Fear

Twitch
Stealth
Great
Wealth

Amber
Eye
Watch
Spy

Nose
Scent
Downwards
Bent

Beauty
Burn
Swiftly
Turn

Den
Cub
Noses
Rub

Quiet rest
For creature best.

Elena Dold (12)
Sale Grammar School

My Thing

Is it a hairclip,
Is it a car?
Is it a pencil case
Or is it a guitar?

Is it a robin,
Is it a dog?
Is it a pussy cat
Or is it a frog?

Is it an aeroplane,
Is it a hat?
Is it a radio
Or is it a rat?

In actual fact,
The thing I've got,
Is a piece of
Blackpool rock!

Lauren Jeffery-Smith (12)
Sale Grammar School

MAN CITY

Man City are waiting for the right time,
With Paulo Wanchope running down the line.
He crosses the ball into the air,
It hits a defender where he shouldn't dare.
It's off the post and into the net,
Man City, the best you can get.
Man City are the best team,
And I'm surely not having a dream.
We have the best defence in the land,
It's better than any brass band.
The attack is the best,
It's better than all the rest.

James Kendall (12)
Sale Grammar School

LAND AND SEA

The waves of the sea,
the land stretched out
as far as the eye can see.
Mountains high in the sky,
with snow so cold,
a thousand years old.

Land and sea outlive the tree,
outlive the animals,
and outlive me!

Night and day,
land and sea will always be.
But humankind will never live to have the key
the key is to live for eternity.

Camille Tsang (11)
Sale Grammar School

The Holiday

I remember the sea
    With the sun in the sky
Watching the brilliant scarlet kite
    Soar and dive in the air up high

I remember the sand,
    Hot beneath my feet
With people sunbathing on colourful towels
    In the bright sun's blistering heat

I remember the great big sandcastles
    Made by my grandad and me
But the towers of sand came crumbling down
    When the tide came in from the sea

I remember the days in the caravan
    For dinner we had baguettes
Or riding my bike around the campsite
    That I'll never forget.

Andrew Mayne (13)
Sale Grammar School

Birthday

B ecause it's my birthday
I 'd rather stay at home
R ed ribbons would stream and I could party all day
T hough I can hope I have to wait
H ooray my family will shout when I get out of bed
D ad will get the presents
A nd Mum too!
Y et I can't hear anyone!

Andrew Smith (12)
Sale Grammar School

ALONE

The leaves swept along the lonely street.
I felt cold and weak.
I felt trapped in my old world.
I had nowhere to go.
I imagined myself withering away on this desolate street.
My mind whizzed around with thoughts and nightmares.
The wind hovered around my bare legs.
The sound of my footsteps followed me down the road
Creaking with every step I took.
My heart beat as if it was trying to escape
From my frozen chest.
My hands suddenly froze and stopped moving.
How was I going to escape from this terror?

Rebecca Griffiths (12)
Sale Grammar School

LIFE

Life . . . I dread it.
People these days are so pathetic.
Trying to fit in,
I wasted three years of my life doing that.
I put on this fake smile to satisfy all of you
If that's not enough, what else can I do?
How much more do you think I can take?
How much longer until I break?
What's the point of living in a life where you constantly feel sad?
This is the life I wish I never had.

Catherine Hay (12)
Sale Grammar School

A TRAIN JOURNEY

The breaks released with a deafening screech,
The smell of the smoke puffing from the choked chimney,
The chattering of the people around me,
But I had no knowledge of them,
I was in a world of my own.

Outside, through the window the surroundings flashed past,
Like an old fashioned, flickering film.

Suddenly the country ended and the polluting city began,
The towering buildings like huge buildings, like mountains
Keeping an eye on what's going on below.

The hustle and bustle of angry car drivers trying to reach work,
The beeping of horns,
The growing of disturbed engines,
Like a group of angry bears fighting for the female.

In an instant we were meandering through the hills
Like a river twisting through the countryside.

When all turned black nothing was to see,
All I could make out was the quick dashes of light,
Glinting in the darkness.
I felt the uncertainty of the darkness.

In a blink of the eye the darkness ended
And the relentless journey came suddenly to a halt,
I returned to Earth.

Ben Bristowe (11)
Sale Grammar School

A Question Left Unanswered

A thick blanket,
Resting over thoughts,
Needing no emotion,
Blocking all recognition.

A dull, smothered yearning,
To live once again,
A need for no attention,
For mind to own body.

A question left unanswered,
A train with no station,
A fearful apprehension,
For when the time does come.

A clock without its chimes,
A tunnel with no end,
As soon it will be judgement day,
A life laid in fate's hands.

Sonya Ratty (12)
Sale Grammar School

The Truth Hurts

Tears stream down my face,
My mascara mildly moves down my face.
Hurtful words are thrown at me like a dagger,
And they stab me in the heart.
The sharp tongue pricks me painfully,
And makes me sob silently.
As I stare at my feet,
Teardrops fall to the ground with a splash.
This person doesn't understand,
How much they are hurting me.

But then on the other hand,
Is it the truth?
All these hurtful words
Could be making me upset because,
I know deep inside me,
That they are the truth.
I suppose I'm just going to have to face the fact
That the truth hurts sometimes.

Alex Hammond (13)
Sale Grammar School

A Refuge Poem

The night is quiet,
As still as it can be.
There is nowhere else to go,
Except where you feel safe.

You are near your refuge place,
Of which you feel you're safe.
The night has lead you the way,
But now you must be on your way to be safe.

The time has finally come,
You are where you feel safe.
Come in and look around,
And you will soon feel safe.

You now feel calm and safe,
Which means this is your place of refuge.
You know now that you can be safe here,
You can come now and again if you do not feel safe.

This is now your refuge of safety.

Kimberley Willott (13)
Sale Grammar School

DREAM OF GLORY

Scoring a goal is a dream.
Scored the perfect goal in last night's dream,
The hero of the winning side,
The finest player in my team.
Scream for the ball,
Loudest player in my team.
Finally took my chance,
No matter what the defenders said,
Offside . . . no!
The perfect goal it was.
Creamed the first division team,
And booted the ball so fast,
The keeper had no chance,
I'm the quickest,
A golden goal it was.
Dream of glory!
The ball flew in,
Dream of glory!
The winner's cup I saw,
Hoping to lift with a glorious shout of,
My dream of glory!

Barry James (13)
Sale Grammar School

THE SUN

A great ball of fire, burning high,
To get to it, you must fly.

A great ball of fire, generating heat,
So hot, in a second, it could burn meat.

A great ball of fire, making light,
It could damage your eyes, it might.

A great ball of fire, really a star,
From the Earth, it is so far.

Mark Jennings (11)
Sale Grammar School

My Busy Life

My life is kind of hectic,
I never have the time,
To sit alone and think,
And make my poem rhyme.

I have a busy schedule,
No time to fit you in,
My social life is going down,
No time to even sin.

From time to time I need to show,
My face among the crowd,
To keep up my appearances,
So they know I'm still around.

My diary is completely full,
For every single day,
No time to spend out with my friends,
I'm always far away.

My time for this is up,
I am afraid to say,
I must get on, I'm running late,
For time I'd really pay.

Houdah Al-Hakim (13)
Sale Grammar School

TV

BBC1 versus ITV
What a great fight, you must agree
Then there's the extra channel 4, channel 5
Only a few programmes keep them alive

Bring on the soaps - EastEnders and Brookie
Watch them all, you might get lucky
The characters are miserable all of the time
Affairs, murders and lots of crime

We'll move onto Saturday with morning TV
I prefer Ant and Dec, but that's just me
There's also the Saturday Show that's new on the box
Miss it, miss out - set your alarm clocks

We mustn't forget the sport, sometimes cricket or footy
Some of the fans you see, God, aren't they nutty
For some of the goals you just have to say wow
They think it's all over - it is now!

Children's TV - it's just so cheesy
I could do their job no problem, dead easy
A lot of new programmes are really boring
If I had to watch them I'd definitely be snoring

Something I'd like to forget but I can't is the news
It's all full of politics and people moaning their views
It's on every channel at least three times a day
It would be once a week if I had my way

So what would I do without good old TV
The person who invented it must be cleverer than me
I watch religiously every night after school
Anybody who doesn't is a bit of a fool!

Emily Mason (11)
Sale Grammar School

My Garden Visitors

One day I looked over the window ledge
When I heard a rustling in the hedge
A black button nose suddenly appeared
And then some eyes and then some ears

Its face like a mouse
Uses twigs to build its house
The squirrel comes and begs at the door
Seeking nuts, it holds out its paw

A small, prickly creature I saw one night
In the light of the moon shining bright
It was searching for slugs with its nose like a spear
But when I drew closer it curled up in fear

The small robin's breast is ruby-red
It comes to my garden to feed on bread
Every winter we hear its song
We listen in pleasure all day long

The fox moved stealthily up my lawn
Returning to its den at the crack of dawn
As it rapidly sped away
It gave its bushy tail a little sway

In the blackbird's nest she sits on her young
I listened in delight as the little birds sung
One by one they left the nest
Now the poor mother can have a rest!

Creatures are big, creatures are small
Creatures are short, creatures are tall
Whatever the size I love them all
From the sly red fox to the snail on my wall.

Diane Johnston (11)
Sale Grammar School

GIRLS

Some are small and some are tall
They are boring and sometimes very adoring

Some are pretty and some are witty
They sometimes lie and they also cry

Some tell you to take a hike while others tell you to hop on your bike
They like to gossip and some are gothic

But when it comes down to girls
You can't live with them
And you can't live without them.

Thomas Edmondson (12)
Sale Grammar School

STARRY NIGHT

What is a star?
I sometimes cry.
A jewelled glint in Heaven's eye?
A silver star 'pon silver screen,
The focus of so many dreams?
I wish, I wish that I could be,
Set apart from here - reality.
The humdrum of my daily life,
Family troubles, classroom strife.
But that - alas, is not to be,
I am stuck in my reality.
I am not a star,
And I often cry.
Not a jewelled glint in Heaven's eye.
Not silver star 'pon silver screen.
The things I can but only dream.

Maya McCourt (13)
Sale Grammar School

JEREMY'S SHOCK!

Deep in the swamps of Harley Barn, Kent,
An old man called Jeremy never paid his rent.
He lived in a shack of darkness and mystery,
He had no future and a lack of history.
People wondered how he ever survived,
Only eating stodge and rats burnt alive.
Then one day he came across something strange and weird,
An old skeleton skull with half a head.
So he said to the skull, 'How are you dead?'
The skeleton said, 'I lost half my head.'
Jeremy said in a fearful voice,
'How did you get in my dirty old place?'
The skull replied, 'I am the walking dead!'
So Jeremy grabbed his shoes and fled.

Martin Smith (13)
Sale Grammar School

THE SUN

The bright white ball in the sky,
Shining up there so high.

People use your shapes in arts and craft,
People use you to light their paths.

Making darkness go away,
You make the night stay away.

You make the moon light up the night,
You make birds able for flight.

The moon comes and scares you away,
So you may rise the next day.

Maisam Lamsehdi (11)
Sale Grammar School

Night

Day is done,
Night is here,
Look at the murky sky,
Stars suddenly appear,
The moon is bright,
Such a pretty sight,
Silver, shining in the sky,
Like the rarest crystal ever found,
Sometimes I see evil demons in the night,
Then I realise they are only shadows giving me a fright,
The grumbling, gusty wind outside,
Is like a monster baring his teeth,
I'm warm and snug,
Tucked up in bed,
Whilst outside in the cold,
Birds fluff their feathers to keep warm,
How I wish that morning would soon arrive,
To watch the moon set and the sun rise,
When morning is getting near,
I'll give a cheer,
As soon I'll be outside,
Under the burning sun once again,
For now I'll sleep,
As I feel quite weak.

Laura Bates (12)
Sale Grammar School

Heaven

Heaven is a place where there is peace and tranquillity
And everyone has equal ability.

Heaven is a place where good people go,
And give off a bright, white, sparkling glow.

Heaven is a place where there is no bad
But instead everyone is happy and glad.

Heaven is a place where I wish to go
But I want my time on Earth to go very slow.

Joshua Sherry-Brennan (11)
Sale Grammar School

I Think I'm Allergic To Exercise

I think I'm allergic to exercise,
What I tell you holds no lies.
Give me a book any time,
I'll even try to make it rhyme.
I hate the stuff -
And I'm no bluff . . .
So please don't be mean,
I'll even give my room a clean.
When I run I huff and puff,
And usually I'm dead tough.
But when I try to hit a ball,
It just won't do as I call.
The basketball never seems to score,
It appears to be like hitting the door.
So doctor, doctor, please help me,
I think I've been stung by the lazyitis bee.

Seonaid Jones (13)
Sale Grammar School

CHRISTMAS

It's Christmas again, my favourite day,
It's the one day of the year when I get my own way,
My perfect Christmas Day is when the snowflakes are falling,
But one Christmas Day was really appalling,
Hardly any snow had fell in the night,
So when I woke up there was little in sight.

The Christmas tree stands towering above me,
Sometimes I think I must be a flea,
All the presents are nestled beneath,
With bells and candles and even a wreath,
The star on top stands proud and bright,
Resembling Bethlehem on that peaceful night.

The presents all neat, stacked under the tree,
Soon to be opened with shouts of glee,
'Oh . . . socks again from Auntie Vee!'
My sister yelling, 'Which one's for me?'
The unwrapping's done, the dinner's cooked,
We're ready to eat now, the turkey's been plucked.

There's one thing to say, the day isn't dull . . .
Not with all these crackers to pull.

David Curran (11)
Sale Grammar School

I LIKE IT!

I like it when I am tucked up in bed,
With a mug of hot chocolate and a big fluffy pillow behind my head.

I like it when it's nice and quiet,
Not when there's a great loud riot.

I like it when I go out with my friends,
We fall out, but make amends.

I like it when my mum gives me kisses and hugs,
When she tells me she loves me very much.

Joe McNulty (11)
Sale Grammar School

SHE ALWAYS GETS WHAT I WANT

She always gets what I want,
Clothes, jewellery, CDs,
Her parents are stinking rich,
She walks around as if she's the queen.

Every boy looks at her,
With her hair up tight.
The teachers all love her,
She thinks she's very bright.

Do you know what?
She stole my best friends.
I cannot believe it!
Now they've turned into 'fashion freaks'
But I know they always pretend.

I really want that necklace of hers,
I'm going to steal her rings.
I so need those shoes of hers,
Then I'll be the queen.

I'm not going to admit it!
No you can't make me.
Fine, then get your own way,
Okay, I'm really jealous, so what?

Eleanor Riley (11)
Sale Grammar School

The Beach

As I walk along the sand,
Flip-flops slapping my heels,
The sun is blazing hot,
The sea is as clear as crystal.
Seagulls are crying,
I can smell the salty sea,
Parasols are still,
The beach is silent.

No breeze,
Just heat.
No sound,
Silence.

The waves are stiller than glass,
Silence.
The children fall asleep,
Silence.
A dolphin whines,
Still silence.

No shops,
Just beach.
No sound,
Silence.

Zara Wiles (12)
Sale Grammar School

The Trouble With You Is . . .

'The trouble with you is,' my best friend said,
And that's when I knew there was trouble ahead,
Our arguments all started with that same opening line,
Not stupid, smelly, silly or swine,
But always, 'The trouble with you is . . . '

We screamed and we shouted,
And bellowed and cried but
The argument just went on,
Neither of us were going to give up our pride,
Because of 'The trouble with you is . . . '

Danny Sudbury (12)
Sale Grammar School

And So The Pen Wrote

And so the pen wrote,
The ink flowed out of the narrow nib,
Covering the snow-white paper with unique blue letters,
Gracefully curving and twisting,
Writing the ever appearing words as they came.

And so the pen wrote,
Scarlet dragons breathed their stunning fire,
Dark, damp dungeons came into play,
Valiant heroes and dastardly villains fought to the end,
Make believe stories of fantasies became a real world,
Unreal becomes as real as the creator.

And so the pen wrote,
Dull roses became scarlet red,
The gleaming sunshine became a glistening yellow,
The soft green springy grass became a variety of different greens,
The calm, huge lake became a smooth aquamarine.

And so the pen wrote,
Forming an attractive title,
Creating storylines as fast as they came,
Making rhyme and beating rhythm,
And so the pen wrote,
This poem you see before you.

Alexander Mann (13)
Sale Grammar School

ZODIAC

Aries: I'm Aries, the ram, my wool, white as can be,
this star sign this week says, 'Move on. Let go. Be free!'

Taurus: Taurus, the bull, this might be the best
to be born to this star sign,
with a sense of recognition you have been blessed.

Gemini: Gemini, we're twins, you'll have said this yourself,
Pluto speaks now, 'Be honest with yourself.'

Cancer: Cancer the crab, this might not sound nice;
this week you require information and advice!

Leo: I'm Leo, the lion, my pride is my roar,
do not take action till you're 100 percent sure!

Virgo: Virgo, the woman, while under pressure, don't crack,
with unnecessary fuss and bother,
'get into it' or be wise and stand back.

Libra: I'm Libra, the scales,
if the odds don't weigh out, then don't be shy,
'be heroic' you're asked by the sky.

Scorpio: I'm Scorpio, the scorpion with a sting in the tail
Mercury's link to Pluto means need for a serious 'done deal'.

Sagittarius: Sagittarius, the archer,
Mars has left the Sagittarius just now.
A new relaxed era, starts here and now.

Capricorn: I'm Capricorn, the goat, you know Mars brings stress,
Mars has entered to Capricorn, so try to relax, I guess.

Aquarius: Aquarius, the water-carrier,
the information you've been missing is here,
there's no universal solution,
but your 'problem' is not as bad as you fear.

Pisces: Pisces, the fish, the world's full of idiots,
you feel you're in a pit
so it's a good job you're a charming sweet fellow, isn't it?

Steven Meyer (12)
Sale Grammar School

My First Day At School

As I walked in, the size swallowed me up like a huge, hairy monster,
Everything was big, even the cage for Pumpkin, the guinea pig
took me by surprise.
There were big kids running round like headless chickens
And tiny little kids, like me, hiding away behind our mums and dads,
When suddenly, from out of nowhere, a bell starting ringing,
All the children hurried inside like hungry bees all charging
for a pot of honey.
I walked inside, found my coat peg and sat on the 'Elephants' table.
My teacher gave us all a sticker, she called our names out,
It came to mine, 'Laura Mannion,' my teacher called out.
What should I say? I didn't really know, so I copied everyone else,
'Yes Miss Birchall,' I called out in a nervous voice.
We then learnt a new song.
Then the bell started ringing, time for lunch,
I went and got my new lunchbox, ate my sandwiches,
And went back to my chair.
Our teacher read us a story about a caterpillar,
The bell rang again and made me jump,
I saw my mum and ran outside to tell her about my first day at school.

Laura Mannion (12)
Sale Grammar School

MONDAY ITIS

There's something about those Mondays that I don't like,
There's something about those Mondays that isn't quite right,
A cough or a cold you can guarantee . . .
. . . you certainly won't be seeing me!
The rest of the week's fine for me,
(Probably cos I don't have double PE!)

Probably those Monday blues
But somehow I happen to lose . . .
. . . my shirt, pens and books,
Tuesday, you teachers don't 'alf give me funny looks,
I don't quite understand . . .
. . . I gave in a note, which Mummy wrote by hand!

I . . . I catch up my work and try my very best,
But still you teachers are such a pest!
Somehow I just happen to 'stand out',
Which makes you teachers ball and shout,
Whatever I do I just can't please you
And that's why I get those good old 'Monday blues'!

Clair Moran (12)
Sale Grammar School

GHOSTS

I slowly but surely trudged to the door,
I opened it, the light, I could no more,
These noises had got me lured,
Miaow! The cat suddenly purred.

The creek from the kitchen,
The gasp from the garden,
The swoosh from the stairs,
It made me realise,
I don't want to be here no more!

I run for the living room,
Nobody there,
Should I run for the stairs?
Don't even dare.

The creek from the kitchen,
The gasps from the garden,
The swoosh from the stairs,
It made me realise,
I don't want to be here no more!

Jonathan Woodall (13)
Sale Grammar School

War, What Is It For?

War, war, war,
What is it for?
War, war, war,
We shouldn't have them anymore.

Some fight for their religion,
They have blinkered vision.
Some fight because of race,
They all have a human face.
Some fight for power,
They want people to fear and cower.
Some fight for their belief,
They can provide no world relief.

Whatever reason, right or wrong,
War doesn't make their case strong.
Does war create a murderer or a hero?
War only creates eternal sorrow.
War only creates devastation and destruction,
Surely parley would create more construction.

Sabah Khan (14)
Sale Grammar School

Reality TV

Surfing through the programmes,
Reality TV.
How much can they throw at us
Until they finally see?

First it was Big Brother,
Then Castaway and crew.
Shipwrecked and Survivor,
And Big Brother Two.

2001 was the birth of Popstars,
Soapstars copied next.
Now we wait for Pop Idol,
Where we put them to the test.

These programmes do become quite boring,
And I just cannot see,
Why these people follow them,
But I'm afraid that is me.

Tuning in for every episode,
Timing is the key.
Watching all the re-runs,
That is the power of reality TV.

Sally Daniels (13)
Sale Grammar School

Bird's-Eye View

Fields, yellow and green, like patchwork,
All different shapes and sizes,
Bushes attaching them together like stitches.

Blue and curvy like the S,
The rivers and lakes go on for miles,
The Ss joining up together.

Forest looking like little spots of green ink,
Fields like patchwork,
Bushes like stitches,
Rivers and lakes like Ss,
Going on, on, on and on, forever.

Gemma Shaw (11)
Sale Grammar School

THE FOOTBALL

It was a hurricane,
Swinging round and round.
With only stadium to play in,
It made a deafening sound.

It was being bounced and bumped,
Thrashed and thwacked.
We all thought
Soon it will have cracked.

Aimlessly kicked,
All of the time.
The crowd cried hooray,
When it crossed the goal line.

The game suddenly stopped,
The ball got a break.
Some players lined up,
But the dive was a fake.

The whistle was blown,
For the end of the game.
The stadium was emptied,
It wasn't the same.

Peter Albin (13)
Sale Grammar School

My Special Holiday

I remember the sunset
The beautiful staggering sun drowning in the sea
The waves
Clashing and dancing in the rhythm of the wind
The warm and soft sand
Sinking and caving in my feet.

I remember the night
The warm, breezy night
The beautiful, fantastic fairy lights hanging from branches of trees
I look up at them
As I swing on the hammock dreaming.

I remember the warm, jolly faces
Filled with laughter as they ate their meals around the pool
The cold, fluttering, fantasy breeze from the sea
Perform tiny ripples in the pool.

I remember the mornings
The warm, breezy mornings
As I could smell the fresh cut fruit
The salty sea
As waves crashed and clanged against the cliffs.

I will always remember this holiday
And always look back
Remembering the last view
From my flight
Of the beautiful, exotic island.

Anuradha Bhabutta (13)
Sale Grammar School

ON SATURDAY MORNING

On a Saturday morning,
At seven o'clock,
I get out of bed,
And go to the shop.

To do my paper round,
As quick as I can,
I use my bike,
Then meet up with Dan.

We go to the park,
And build up a jump,
So we can practise,
Our most amazing stunt.

It's time for lunch,
We both go home,
To fill our stomachs,
So we don't moan.

After lunch,
I call for Dave,
So we can go out,
With the money we've saved.

I spot a garment in the shop,
I try it on and wonder what,
It is a red Lee Cooper top,
I saw the price and got a shock.

Daryl Rayner (14)
Sale Grammar School

Starlight

Starlight, starlight
Wish upon a star tonight
See a star so far away
Grab it quick and make it stay

See it glisten in your hand
So small as grains of sand
Like a diamond and precious too
I can't believe it, but it's true

I found it in the silver skies
Deep where the moon lies
Drifting towards me to reach the ground
Slowly, softly, not making a sound

But now it's sizzling out aloud
Soaring, howling like a hound
But give it time to let it weep
And slowly let it fall asleep

If you believe in it you would come
And see what the star had done
So I'll wait here until the day
You yourself will pass this way.

Zara Schofield (13)
Sale Grammar School

Champions

The puck drops at the face-off
He passes it back to the D man
He skates with the puck and trips over his foot
The other team get possession

The forward collects the puck
And shoots with all his might
He hits the netminder on the head
He falls into the net
And throws the puck in the goal
Storm score!

Philip Harrison (11)
Sale Grammar School

DEATH

Death is cold,
As cold as ice and arctic winds.
Death is quick,
Quick and unexpected.
Death is invisible,
However, it is fatal and devastating.
Death is painful,
Just like a pin piercing through skin.
Death is tasteless,
Nevertheless, it tastes sickening in your throat.
Death is quiet,
So quiet you can hear a pin hitting the floor.
Death is mad,
It is crazy, just like a deranged psychopath.
Death is sad,
It makes you weep in its pleasure.
Death is an exit,
It concludes your life.
Death is vile,
It looks horrific and has no feelings.

Death is evil!

Christopher Kelsall (13)
Sale Grammar School

THE HULK

We're waiting at the bottom, nervous as we wait,
As we walk up to the entrance, we join the queue,
Looking high into the sky - the Hulk we're about to ride.
The carriages await, it's our turn next,
Dreading this moment we clamber into our seats,
We set off through the tunnel.
Slowly we approach the opening, waiting like a huge open mouth,
And we see the ground below.
Underneath a net, drooping like a hammock,
Saving caps and sunglasses from plummeting to earth,
Belonging to riders who carelessly forgot to remove them.
There is no turning back as we shoot out at 60mph,
Like a viper's tongue.
Up and down, inside out, loop the loop,
As we twirl upside down,
Stomachs churning, our heads dizzy.
Everything flashes past like a video on fast forward,
Rapidly we approach the end of the track - thank goodness it is over.
Stopping abruptly, our knuckles white as ghosts,
We gripped on so tightly.
Slowly we unpeel our clammy fingers from the metal bar,
Alighting from the carriage, our legs wobbling,
We walk away . . . 'Where's the next ride?'

Megan Armson (12)
Sale Grammar School

A Typical Morning

I woke up this morning surprised to find
That I had a million things on my mind
Have I done the homework? It's in for today
Oh well, if I ignore it, it should go away
But wait, I need to brush my hair
Why is life so hard? It really isn't fair
I go to the bathroom, but do I get in?
No, my brother's in there, so I decide to make a din
'Let me in, you've been in there too long!'
He didn't hear me, he was trying to sing a song
It's quarter to eight, and I'm still not dressed
Oh dear, school gets you so distressed
I get in the bathroom, I do what I need
I'd forgotten there was someone to feed
Myself of course, oh I don't have time
I'll miss breakfast today, it isn't a crime
I get my books for the day ahead
Then I remembered the book I should have read
My mind yet again is spinning around
I try and calm down without making a sound
I let out a scream from where I lay
Only to find it was Saturday.

Sarah Alcock (12)
Sale Grammar School

I Only Wish It Could Be Our Team That Won

There is a chance we're going to win
If all our shots go in!
This team were unlucky to lose
Our missed shots were greeted with boos!

Our team is looking so poor -
They were extremely lucky to draw -
Dave was the only player with some skill -
All the rest of the team had nil.

The opposition tried all to score
As the match went on even more
The goalie made an amazing save -
His hands grabbed the ball like a cave.

All of our players were in despair!
Now the manager has no hair
The final goal went in -
How sweet it is to win!

I only wish it could be our team that won!

Nathan Bullock (13)
Sale Grammar School

The Ghost

I was in a house
When I heard a noise
A creaking door
Or a scary ghost?

I went to look
And something moved
I went to look
And saw a ghost!

It wasn't very scary
Although it wanted to be
It wanted to scare people
So I let it scare me!

Robert Starling (12)
Sale Grammar School

WEATHER

Rain
Dark and dismal, damp in the air
Clammy and close, with distant rumbles to be heard
Fork lightning awakens the sky
Yes! I need a raincoat

Sun
Bright and inviting, warmth in the air
Clear blue cloudless sky
Sun-warmed sea stretching afar
Better go to the beach

Wind
Whistling through the trees
Flags flapping in the wind
Leaves twisting and twirling
Coats fastened high

Snow
A single bird's footprint in the snow
Cold, crunchy and new
Picking up the soft, crisp snow, freezing your fingers
Let's finish that snowman.

Peter McGuckian (12)
Sale Grammar School

BONFIRE NIGHT

The stars were shining bright
It was a cold, dark night
All was quiet and still
When all of a sudden
Out of its cave came a
Red, orange and golden
Dragon
It slowly uncurled itself
Releasing red, white, yellow
Green, blue, purple, pink sparks
Into the sky, they whirled, they twirled
Twisted and flew across the sky
The dragon's flames were crackling
Then at that moment all went quiet
The coloured sparks had faded away
The dragon lumbered back into its cave
The stars were shining bright
Something extraordinary happened that night.

Lisa Pauley (11)
Sale Grammar School

MY GARDEN IN WINTER

My garden, leaves crinkly and brown,
Blowing about in this busy old town.
Trees all around us, no leaves, all bare,
No birds trying to make nests from old pieces of hair.

Birds stop looking for worms in the ground,
They're all hiding in the compost mound.
Grass going all frosty, so, so cold,
Killing off flowers which are very old.

A blanket of snow came at night,
Making my garden ever so bright.
Snowmen are made by my brother the next day,
All the cold weather ruins the rabbit's hay.

Robert Williams (12)
Sale Grammar School

THE HIPPO

There they stand in a group together
bum to bum in the muddy weather.
With their mouths as wide as a bus,
they gulp anything in one, with no fuss.

They stand so lonely, lazy and slow,
all because he's a big hippo.
They look so dainty under the water,
as along the riverbed they saunter.

Then there is an accidental nudge,
but the other hippo does not budge.
He swings his head so very fast,
it attacked the other with such a blast.

It all kicks off so furiously,
some join, others leave curiously.
As they each collide with a bash,
the river is making such a splash.

They fight and fight until one gives in,
when they win they feel good within.
It all calms down, end of show,
there they stand so lazy and slow.

Lisa McDonald (13)
Sale Grammar School

MEMORIES

'Oft in the stilly night,
Ere slumber's chain has bound me,
Fond memory brings the light,
Of former days around me.'

I see a shiny convertible,
Navy blue with a jet-black roof,
It drives like a 'Eurostar' train,
And is as cool as an icy-cold cube.

I see some kittens in a farm,
Their faces with eyes closed like slits,
One could fit in the palm of my hand,
Vulnerable they are in the dark.

I see a picture in a book,
'Sunflowers', by Vincent van Gogh,
The yellow colour makes me rise with joy,
The petals like a mane of a lion.

Tom Howorth (11)
Sale Grammar School

WHEN I GO ON HOLIDAY

When I go on holiday
I sit there in the sun,
While my sisters play in the pool
And have loads and loads of fun.
They are going down water slides
And jumping in and out,
While I sit and watch them
Feeling really left out.

I finally awake from a long relaxing sleep,
I get up from the chair with a great big leap.
I walk towards the steps and dive into the pool,
The water is refreshing, relaxing and cool.
I then run towards the water slides,
I fight my way to the top,
Before I know it, in no time at all,
I land with a great big *plop!*

Jade Clarke (12)
Sale Grammar School

BULLY

A bully has nasty ways
In everything he does or says,
A bully isn't really cool,
Anyone can make someone feel like a fool,
The bully thinks that he is smart
Yet he is only someone with a very cold heart,
The bully has an awful greed,
To be so nasty is just one of his needs,
A bully is a nobody,
And neither you, neither me
Should ever listen to a bully,
So don't just keep it locked inside,
Tell somebody with whom you confide,
And even if this does not do,
Remember -
The bully is the one with the problem,
Not you!

Jennifer Worrall (13)
Sale Grammar School

TIGER

Powerful predator, careful hunter,
Hidden in dense undergrowth.
Coat as rich as a king's robe,
Colours in all their majesty.
Thick, warm fur.
Camouflage and protection against a Siberian winter.
Strong flaming orange or purest white,
Alternating with marvellous black.
White spotted ears.
Pads through the jungle,
Not lumbering, but with utmost awareness.
Ears pricked, careful not to make the slightest sound.
Though big and strong; gentle and caring,
Looks after cubs as well as any mother,
Only strikes for survival and defence.

Leila Hill (12)
Sale Grammar School

AUTUMN

Autumn is coming nearer,
And the air is getting colder,
The trees are drooping in the chilling air,
And the leaves are falling gracefully to the ground,
The leaves are browner and the weather is worse,
As summer draws to a closing end,
The wind is stronger, pushing anything over,
As everything is getting damper and colder,
So as autumn awaits us,
And the nights start to get darker,
We enter a new season,
A new season of freezing weather and scary nights.

Ryan Wise (12)
Sale Grammar School

THE THREE LITTLE WOLVES

My beloved dears you are old enough now,
to go out and work and do yourselves proud.

Be good little wolves and look after yourselves,
buy all your building materials off the good little elves.

The first little wolf went to a young elf,
and asked for some materials that would be good for himself.

He piled them up in a huge great stack,
and paid the elf with corn in sacks.

He built day and night and never stopped,
only until he felt his brain had popped.

The other two wolves were naughty and silly,
and went to the goblins who were up in the valley.

They asked the goblins for materials they had,
but they cheated the wolves, they were faulty and bad.

Surely enough the big bad pig came,
the cute little wolves were his best aim.

He sadly stamped on the silly two,
and the big bad pig made a tasty stew.

And yet he moved onto the first little wolf,
who was honest and truthful and never told off.

The wise little wolf had a trick up his sleeve,
he decided to make a lasso he could weave.

He lured the stupid pig into his trap,
and lassoed him down with a sharp slap.

The wolf ate the pig on that night,
but boy did he put up a fight.

Ellis Bailey-Cross (11)
Sale Grammar School

MR TOOSOP'S SHOE SHOPS

Mr Toosop
Had a shoe shop
In the heart of town.
A joyous man, was Mr Toosop,
You never saw him frown.

Then one cold night,
Out of spite,
The shoe shop was burnt down.
'I'll buy a new shop'
Sobbed Mr Toosop
In the outskirts of town.

So off to buy a new shop
Went Mr Toosop,
He looked all over town.
'A clothes shop, toy shop,
What will I buy?'
Oh how he felt a clown!

Then Mr Toosop
Saw a shoe shop
'For sale' it read on the door.
He went right in
And made a bid
And got more than he bargained for.

The shop had four floors
With a painted front door
And beautifully carpeted floors.
He shouted, 'I'm happier than ever before,
I'll have to buy some more!'

From then on Mr Toosop
Bought more shoe shops
Scattered all across town.
Toosop's shoe shops
Were his shoe shops
The most popular shoe shops around!

Hayley Griffiths (12)
Sale Grammar School

War And Peace

War and peace are of opposite meanings
People make war a sight of red blood Hell
While peace can be found in a wishing well.
To drop a penny comes the wish
Those innocent soldiers had one last kiss.
War is cruel and full of guns
Peace is a place where people are free.

War is just disharmony that spits and kills
The injured men upon the hills.
The cordite smoke fills the air and gives pollution.
Peace is calm like ocean waves
Rage is anger rushing through
The sky of clouds and sunny blue.

With a poppy wreath beneath your arm
Just remember the men that died
Be very patient and very calm.
Peace has no pain
Let's hope that war will never strike again.

Sophie Long (11)
Sale Grammar School

Darkness

A deep shadow lurks in the rough darkness
Bringing home fear and apprehension.
A satin cloak of black, that shields eyes from unwanted sights.
The thought of what goes on when there is no light.

The night creeps on and you fear of new dangers.
What's round the next frightening corner of your nightmare?
More terrible experiences coming your way?

You try to escape, but there's nowhere to go,
You're trapped in this prison of darkness and fear.

Rachel Garland (12)
Sale Grammar School

My Dream

I have a wonderful dream,
I always will have.
One day that dream won't be a dream,
It will be real.

That dream is important,
Is it my life.
That dream is happening now,
I am determined to succeed.
My dream is special, it is mine,
I will win that dream all through my life.
It will happen I know it, I feel it,
I dream it.

Jodie Murphy (13)
Sale Grammar School

GHOST FRIEND

As we moved into our new house a visitor did appear,
But I was the only one who could see him, I was shaking with fear.
If I tried to hide he would find me and never go away,
No matter how hard or much I did pray.

I asked him what he wanted, so he led me to a book,
I think he was indicating for me to have a look!
As I opened the book I saw spell after spell,
I wondered if this ghost was from Heaven or Hell!

Suddenly the pages flew and flew,
Until they opened and settled on page 122.
The title of the spell was 'Lie A Ghost To Rest',
I did not know what to do, what would be best?

I decided after a while to read out all of the spell,
This would prove whether the ghost was from Heaven or Hell!
As I read I was shaking like never before,
And I wondered if all this was against the law!

As I finished reading aloud, nothing happened at first,
But, then out of the book a spray of purple dust did burst.
I heard screams and shouts, I was in a state of shock,
Suddenly on the attic door there came a loud knock!

Just in time the spray of purple dust did disappear,
And I could feel that the ghost was nowhere near!
I ran to the attic door and who should be waiting there?
My mother, with a message from under the bottom stair.

It read, 'Thank you very much, I now feel a lot better,'
I saw my mother's face, but could not explain the letter!
I went to bed early that night, dreaming happy dreams,
As I knew my grateful ghost friend was at rest now, it seems!

Gina Chiarelli (12)
Sale Grammar School

SEPTEMBER 11TH 2001

Resentfulness, anguish and pain,
When will these people realise that this is no game?
Victims in the ground suffer,
All so desperate to find their lover.

Sweeping, sustained and effective,
Help is hard at work.
The sunken souls of the traumatised city,
Stand silent with disbelief.

Satanic, infernal and devious,
Who would have known that a political battle of hatred
Would lead to such insanity?
When one family is weeping for the loss of a relation,
Why is the other one laughing?

Democracy, terrorism and freedom,
What grief and sadness one act can cause,
One world united due to the same devastation.
Why can we not join together as a nation?

Eve Parker (13)
Sale Grammar School

THE RESCUER

He lies asleep,
Although his eyes are closed, his expression is troubled,
All around him sirens wail and the air is thick with smoke,
From his head to his heavy boots, he is coated in dust,
His fireman's helmet lies by his side as he tries to rest,
His bed is a dirty sleeping bag in-between the scaffolding,
Which holds up the crumbling buildings of Manhattan.

Rosie King (13)
Sale Grammar School

A Cold Winter's Night

A fire crackles in the living room
And the wood lies by the axe
All the windows shut tight and secure
So cosy, as the family relax.

The howling wind creeps through the gaps in the windows
But the fire keeps them snug
The smell of home-made mince pies
As the dog sleeps on the rug.

A mug of steaming hot cocoa
Is held tightly in their hands
It's almost time for Santa Claus
And the reindeers to come and land.

Off they go to bed
As the grandfather clock strikes twelve
Little Timmy wonders,
'Where is Santa and his elves?'

Tom Singleton (11)
Sale Grammar School

When I Go To The Orchestra

When I go to the orchestra
The conductor sways
While the music plays
Drums beat the pulse
Cymbals clash deafeningly
Flutes toot victoriously
Trumpets boom smugly
Violins squeak peacefully
When I go to the orchestra.

Nicholas Whitmore (11)
Sale Grammar School

MEMORIES

The low beam clung to the ceiling supporting it
Like a weightlifter heaving his load
The stairs furiously cried for help when you stood on them
As I lay on the empty bed, it was like quicksand was pulling me in.
The room was like an ancient temple
Waiting for many things to be discovered.

I stared at the picture which hung above the dusty fireplace
People were laughing whilst having a picnic
It made me smile with delight
Colours sang in a beautiful soft voice
It was bright with people running around in the fields

The bear sat in the lonely corner waiting to be touched
It felt like bristles on a brush
The arms gripped onto the bear by one thread
The chocolate brown-coloured bear's crystal eyes shined exceedingly.

Rachel Griffiths (11)
Sale Grammar School

A POEM?

Teacher says to write a poem,
About anything we're told,
Anything? What to do?
Hundreds of topics,
Which one to choose?
A poem of animals?
Which to use?
Swordfish? Zebra?
Too many choices,
Which one to use?

Desmond Clarke (12)
Sale Grammar School

AUTUMN FOR ME IS . . .

The sky is a misty blue
With threads of grey too.
A feathery grey,
But only at day.
The wind whistles, whispers and swooshes.

Nests look all snug, but abandoned,
Swallows migrate to countries afar.
Flying away in a massive flock,
While more birds line up in stock,
And robins jump up and down.

Sweet little dormice,
They've eaten all their woodlice.
Now it's time for their hibernation,
But first they've got to track down their location.

The bonfire flames are all dancing,
People are around it, prancing.
The smoke is twirling upward into the sky,
And the sky is lit up by a cascade of fireworks.

The branches of a tree make a silhouette,
While the leaves turn orange and violet.

Fairy toadstools spotted red and white,
Altogether make a lovely sight,
But I cannot touch them.

Harvest time is definitely here,
Picking berries at the end of the year.

This is what harvest is to me.

Lucinda Lea (11)
Sale Grammar School

A Day I'll Never Forget

A day I'll never forget,
Even though I wasn't there.
The day the Twin Towers collapsed.
Collapsed!
Once standing proud amongst the world's most famous buildings.
The skyline in New York will never be the same again.
Instead of the tall towers there was smoke.
Smoke!
Great black clouds of it.
It was chasing the people like a huge monster.
Turning the corners, covering everything in its path.
Thousands dead.
Thousands!
Who did it?
Is this the beginning of the end . . .?

Emma Jamieson (12)
Sale Grammar School

Memories

A small but very playful dog
A dog that never tires
Its wisdom is behind its time
A scruffy coat that's silky smooth
It has no idea it cannot prevail
But its determination drives it on.

The crisp waves quiver as our boat disappears
The speed is magical and for miles on end not a ripple
The deep sea turns grey as the vessel bobs
The sky opens and the rains pour down
A great escape and an unforgettable memory.

A haunting picture with a chilling mood
I see it now, a staring portrait
A grand frame with a thin edge of gold
Its eyes seem to stare at me
Its smile is a wicked thing
It's not an evil smile but still it gets to me.

Jordan Shiels (11)
Sale Grammar School

Memories

Oft' in the stilly night
Ere slumber's chain has bound me
Fond memory brings the light
Of former days around me.

When I was young we owned a cat
He had jet-black and milky-white silky fur
He used to sleep upon his mat
And he had a quiet little purr.

I went to my gran's when I was young
And I read a traditional rhyme book
The musical rhymes I sat there and sung
But one day it was took.

'Twas my auntie's wedding day
Driven in my grandad's beautiful car
So beautiful, I wanted to ask
If we may go for a ride far.

All these memories I remember well
Like a video tape inside my head
So vivid is my memory
Of all these happy times.

Rosie Hicks (11)
Sale Grammar School

Escape It

School is a place, where you're not really free
You cannot escape,
It's not *my* cup of tea!

Will someone explain the reason of school?
'It's better for children,
Than playing the fool!'

The teachers are mean, the headmaster is too
The children are boring
I can't find the loo!

The doors are in front of my eyes, I can't see
They're opening up
Coming to get me!

My brain isn't working, I want to go home,
I've got stomach ache
I'm all on my own!

I wake up and realise it's Friday, *woo hoo!*
It's weekend tomorrow
Let's plan what to do!

Megan Price (11)
Sale Grammar School

The Air Raid

As I sit in the air raid shelter,
Thoughts walk through my head,
Will I be alive tomorrow?
Will my house still be standing?

As I lie on the top bunk,
Corrugated iron and mud above me,
The Nazi planes flying overhead,
As I think I'm safe, tucked away in the shelter.

I suddenly awake,
To find beams of light streaming in,
I survived last night,
So did my house,
But today's another day.

Sarah Wagstaffe (12)
Sale Grammar School

CHURCH

In the spooky forest, there stands an eerie old church.
Naturally, it's deserted, apart from the scuttling spiders spinning
Their silvery webs, and the little mice scurrying around.
The door hangs miserably by its rusty hinge,
Elegantly stained glass windows grow moss,
As the vibrant colours fade away into the gloom.
The filthy bricks wear away, but are the perfect nest for moths.
Inside this once beautiful church,
There is a deep layer of dust lining the floor.
Despite that, you can just make out the moth-eaten red carpet
Running in and out of each pew, twisting like a slithering snake.
At the altar stands a grimy christening bowl, made from the
Finest white marble, once so proud,
But now looking sorrowful and humiliated.
Pipes above rattle, determined to work full steam once again,
However, they fail terribly and settle back down.
The electrics flicker and scream in pain
As a rat gnaws away at open wires.
Nevertheless, it sounds like things are not too bad, for there are
Lots of excited shouts, laughter and music, a party presumably.
But, as I stroll towards the clamour, everything stopped, the music,
The laughter, the fun, everything fell silent as I came face
To face with nothing but a misty old *graveyard.*

Anna Harvey (12)
Sale Grammar School

The River

The river creeps along gently just like a swan,
The blue water as blue as the summer sky,
It runs silently along the green grassed riverbank,
It runs below the weeping branches of a willow tree.

The deep swirling water has no destination,
The deep swirling water is like a never-ending river,
It never stops and it never slows,
But it can get deeper and deeper,
It can get wider and wider,
Every torrent spells danger,
Every torrent spells fear,
Every torrent spells power,
The river can also be a raging bull,
Like a soldier going into battle,
It is like water being flushed away,
The roaring water rapidly speeds down,
Like a racing car on the track.

Which do you like better,
The swan or the bull?

David Duncan (11)
Sale Grammar School

Memories

Animals/Rabbit
There was a sweet rabbit called Fluffy
She was very white and silky
She used to dig little holes
And then hide in them
She would run down the streets and in people's gardens
Her ears pointed up
And she had a dark black piece of fur in the middle of her body.

Paintings/Pictures
I can vaguely remember a painting on my wall
It had a very weird effect on me
It had been painted in dark colours all over
At night it looked like it was coming out of the painting to get me
It was in front of my bed
Waiting to scare me.

Devika Jalota (11)
Sale Grammar School

My Poem On World War I

The nasty wail of men screaming,
While relatives are crying.
Will they ever come back?
Men dreaming; will they see the light of day?
For dying is the price to pay.
One boot on,
One boot off,
Holding gun in hand,
Listening to the sound of the band,
The band wondering while they play,
Will they suffer the same way?
The flash of light making men blind,
Some of them out of their mind,
Some of them dying,
Others crying.
Men committing suicide,
Others dying for their country with pride.
Bombs, guns, snipers, more,
Ammunition needed for war.
Millions and millions of lives were lost,
That indeed was a very big cost.

Joshua Green (12)
Sale Grammar School

FIRST DAY

My first day at High School, what a change,
No more getting up late every day.

The time is still early and I am barely awake,
Though it feels like rush hour is closing in on me.

I get to the bus stop, yawning and stretching,
The bus is nearly here,
I better get ready.

I arrive at the gates hoping things will be fine,
I walk in taking one step at a time,
I get there, the corridors are big and packed,
I walk down being pushed and barged.

I get to my form room, looking out at the crowd,
It feels so weird not having my friends here,
In comes my form teacher, Mr Roberts is his name
Who gives me the timetable for the year ahead.

The school bell rings, what a relief,
The dining hall's deserted, I am the first in line,
I stare at the sausage, burgers and chips
A good selection, a hard choice.

The school bell rings, it's time to go,
I pack my things in my bag,
Then dash outside to catch the bus,
What a relief, my first day over,
Now I can look forward to tomorrow.

Christopher Hodgkiss (11)
Sale Grammar School

MEMORIES

Sculpture
A gallery I travelled to
On a rainy and foggy day
And I saw a peculiar sculpture of a man's head
On a wall facing me.
A white bath plug was an eye and a shoe was a smile.
It also had some string for an ear.
The sculpture made me feel queasy.
The face had a horrified expression, where is the ghost?

Toy
My old toy was Jemima.
No surprise a duck.
I was two and she was pink and white and grey.
I flapped her wings till they were worn,
But still one day she flew away,
I was devastated.
We searched and searched and finally found her
Nesting behind a comfy floral armchair.

Pet
My aunty had a sheepdog called Jack.
His fur was a hotchpotch of brown, white and black,
His intelligent eyes sparkled,
While his ears pricked at every sound.
If someone came to the door he would lumber along.
Even an old dog can learn new tricks.
I loved that dog although he was old,
I will always miss him, he had a heart of gold.

Sophie Wright (11)
Sale Grammar School

CONFLAGRATION

Confusion sweeps over the once mighty city,
Devouring unfortunate souls.
Obsessive ogres taunt crumbling, scorched buildings.
Never-ending screams and cries fill the pitch-black air.
Ferocious, flickering flames dance and sprint around the desolate city.
Livid, acrid, sparks waltz and dance around the scorched houses.
A shimmer of blaring light glints across the ebony sky.
Gargantuan flames meander from household to household.
Relentless sparks glow and blaze around the shimmering town.
Aggressive, raging buildings burn and flare in the distance.
Tension rises as terrified witnesses
Watch their homes tumble to the stony ground.
Innocent, frightened people scream and cry with distress.
Outbursts of destructive flames dart and dash across the empty city.
Night ends and morning arrives, filled with depression and destruction.

Alex Bullough (12)
Sale Grammar School

BLACK

Deceit and betrayal were stuck to a side,
Eternal guilt follows behind,
It tastes so empty, dull and dark,
That an eerie feeling fills my heart,
Death is poured in,
Leaving a motionless powder,
Nightmares jump out,
With a scream and a shout,
Mournful cries await my soul,
At the end of this sinful hole,
My life is as black as the darkest night sky,
Emptiness rules me, that I can't deny.

Danielle Challis (11)
Sale Grammar School

PETS

Animals of all species
Some are right beasties
Some are cute
Some you wish you could put on mute

Some soft and furry
Others coarse and hairy
Cats are very purry
Frogs are very slimy
Some have straight fur, some have curly

Sometimes they mither
For instance droolers . . . a lot of saliva
Some are playful
Some are careful
But some are very dozy

Some are very funny
A soft, cuddly bunny
Some are very friendly
But some are very scary

Some have scales
Not forgetting big whales
Some have shells
Some have feathers
Some can smell

We love them as they love us back
They would always care and look after us
Someone who listens
Someone to talk to when no one's there
They're our best friends

So which pet would you choose?

Adele Ferrari (12)
Sale Grammar School

MEMORIES

Oft' in the stilly night
Ere slumber's chain has bound me
Fond memory brings the light
Of former days around me.

The metallic green Jaguar
A royal saloon.
Its cream leather seats fit for a queen,
It glides smoothly like a dove in flight,
Rich oak dashboard and thick leather clad steering wheel.

A classic car!

I taste the gorgeous sweet maple syrup,
A cold, smooth, sticky taste, perfect for me.
Great on pancakes, waffles and food like that,
Cool and smooth, I think I could drink some.
The tastiest, most soothing thing that ever, ever
Entered my mouth.
Mmmmm!

Oft' in the stilly night
'Ere slumber's chain has bound me
Fond memory brings the light
Of former days around me.

Thomas Urmston (11)
Sale Grammar School

SCHOOL BLUES

I've got the school blues, got the school blues bad,
It really makes me feel quite mad,
Five days a week is too much for me,
The weekend brings me so much glee.

School sloppy dinners, slop around the plate,
I can't even throw them to my mate!
English, maths and geography too,
Doesn't this sound exciting to you?

Teachers talk and talk and gaggle,
The corridors are filled with children's babble,
PE lessons are a bore,
I really don't want them anymore!
Paper aeroplanes fly around the room,
In the stockroom hides the teacher's broom!

In the morning the big blue bus bounces down the road,
Travelling on the way to school,
The noise is loud but cheery,
As homework is passed from seat to seat.

Woodwork is hard and a bore,
History is such a chore,
At five past three the bell rings loud,
A wave of pupils exit in a crowd,
I've got the school blues bad!

Angharad Ward (12)
Sale Grammar School

THE NIGHT

The sun disappears on the vast horizon.
Night blankets the westerly sky.
The clouds part and awaken each star,
Which twinkle and shine from a distance.
The moon smiles down on our blue planet,
Enlightening the face with its presence.
Sleepy animals appear from their hollows.
The grass sways in the breeze.
Soon the sun will be uncovered,
To arise the new dawn.

Debora Higham (13)
Sale Grammar School

ZODIAC

Look at the stars
And read the signs
Or even the planets in their lines.
From lions to scorpions,
All twelve,
Nobody has none,
Everybody has one.
Way up in space,
Everyone checks in case
Their destiny has changed.
Is it false or true?
Will it do?
Do you believe,
Or don't you?

Lauren Griffin (13)
Sale Grammar School

My Mate Bear

Once I had a teddy bear
A big thing with straight brown hair
He had beady eyes and a rubber nose
Chubby legs and stumpy toes

I put him in my bed at night
And if I got scared I'd hold him tight
We would sit and talk until it was late
I called him Bear, he was my first mate

But one day we were playing, just messing about
When I tore off his leg and the stuffing came out

My mum and dad told me he wasn't okay,
So my best mate Bear was thrown away.

Martin Thelwell (11)
Sale Grammar School

Snow

The trees thick with falling snow,
Falling onto the tip of your toe.
The children playing happily with the snow,
While throwing snowballs to and fro.

Now it's time to go inside,
He said goodbye to his friend,
The snowing stopped, it was the end.

Dominic King (11)
Sale Grammar School

A Starry Night

I'm in my room lying under my bedcovers,
I wriggle, I toss side to side, I just can't get to sleep,
So I sit up in my bed very cautiously,
I look around, I see nothing but pitch-black,
I decide to build up enough courage to look out my window,
I take a quick peep outside my window, I see darkness,
I see the moon, it shines as brightly as brand new cutlery,
I see stars lighting up the sky but yet as small as mice,
I draw the curtains back and lie down in my bed,
I then close my eyes and off I go to sleep.

Gabriel Erturk (12)
Sale Grammar School

Nature

So big, so great
It's something you can't hate
The trees, with all the colours, with all heights
The flowers, so small, yet so bright
The fruits, so lush, so nice
The sky, so close, but so high
The animals, some run, some fly
Some are fierce, some are shy
Some have a melody, some have a cry
So who created all of this?
It was God, the creator of life.

Saman Haider (13)
Sale Grammar School

Ever So High

Up, up high in a skyscraper,
Looking down on the city,
Cars looking like beetles,
Roads like centipedes.

Ever so high in a skyscraper.

High-pitched screams come from the city,
While specks of dust roam the streets,
Matches are lit and an ember
Lights up the city.

Ever so high in a skyscraper.

Cones and squares are houses and chimneys,
Puffing out a thick fog,
Hiding the city in a cloud of smoke,
While I look down.

Ever so high in a skyscraper.

I look down,
I feel tall,
I see the model village,
Ever so high in a skyscraper.

Elizabeth Craven (11)
Sale Grammar School

THE ZODIAC

The ram and a bull, a crab and a lion,
A goat and a fish, a scorpion too -
Are these the creatures you'll find in a zoo?

Gemini, Sagittarius,
Virgo, Aquarius,
These are the people; do you know who's who?

There is an odd one,
An object it is,
These are the scales,
They make up the biz!

Jamie Boucher (12)
Sir Thomas Boteler High School

FISHY, FISHY PISCES

On a day in March,
I make a wish,
Cos I was born,
Under the fish.

This fish is not to be found
In a snack,
It's Pisces,
The third sign of the zodiac.

Chris Roane (12)
Sir Thomas Boteler High School

Space, What Is It Like?

S himmering, shining stars
P lenty of pretty planets
A ce, awesome, asteroids,
C apricorn clowning around
E normous, excellent space.

Jessica Forshaw (11)
Sir Thomas Boteler High School

Space

S is for sparkly stars
P is for pretty planets
A is for amazing asteroids
C is for colourful comets
E is for the exciting eclipses.

Rebecca Boucher (11)
Sir Thomas Boteler High School

The Ram

A is for the *air* I breathe
R is for the *ram* I hunt
I is for the *intelligence* I have
E is for *every* creature I see
S is for the *special* sounds I hear.

Leah Hughes (11)
Sir Thomas Boteler High School

Scorpio

S tinging its prey
C lawing its way along
O rangy-red colour
R ipping its
P rey apart
I in the . . .
O asis.

Robert Kane (11)
Sir Thomas Boteler High School

Taurus

T is for *tulips*
A is for *adoring*
U is for *unforgettable*
R is for *rose*
U is for *ungrateful*
S is for *special.*

Lehann Cain (11)
Sir Thomas Boteler High School

Virgo

V is for *very* good fun
I is for *interesting*
R is for the *respect*
G is for the *gifts* I get
O is for how much I play *outside.*

Danielle Hill (11)
Sir Thomas Boteler High School

AQUARIUS

A is for *air*, the element of Aquarius
Q is for *quite* something that Aquarians aren't
U is for *Uranus*, the ruling planet of Aquarius
A is for *Aquarians*, the people that make Aquarius what it is
R is for *really* original, this is what Aquarians are
I is for *independent,* Aquarians do things on their own
U is for *usually* friendly, Aquarius is the friendliest sign of the zodiac
S is for *sky*, just look up and you will see the sign of Aquarius.

Emma Paternoster (12)
Sir Thomas Boteler High School

ARIES

A is for *adoring* you
R is for *running* a hundred miles to see you
I is for being *inconsistent*
E is for *encouraging* me
S is for *seeing* your beauty.

Johnathan Eden (11)
Sir Thomas Boteler High School

THE SCORPION

Blossom of evil.
Petals of hidden venom.
Beware of the sting.

Lauren Leicester (11)
Sir Thomas Boteler High School

AN AFRICAN DAY

The morning sunshine
Animals wake sleepily
To start a new day

Lions lie fast asleep
Under the golden sunset
Peacefully dreaming

In the pitch-black sky
Stars like twinkling diamonds
The half moon shining.

Rebecca McCartney (11)
Sir Thomas Boteler High School

SPACE

Shooting stars flying
Shining brightly like light bulbs
Travelling through space.

Laura Whitfield (11)
Sir Thomas Boteler High School

LIBRA

Libra is the scales,
Shy, caring, considerate,
Month of October.

Emma Worrall (12)
Sir Thomas Boteler High School

SPACE

The stars are very shiny,
The moon is very bright,
And the stars are around the moon,
They shine at night.

They send up rockets into space,
To explore for the human race,
Exciting things explorers find
But the moon dust they leave behind.

Mars is red,
The sky is blue,
I would love to go to the moon
Would you?

Philip Brown (11)
Sir Thomas Boteler High School

STAR SIGN

A is for being pro-*active*!
Q is the sign of *quality*
U is for *understanding* everyone
A is when you *admire* someone
R is when you *respect* others
I is for *intelligence* from your brain
U is for being *unique* all the time
S is for the *special* thing that always stays with you.
Aquarius!

Shahnaz Malik (11)
Sir Thomas Boteler High School

Signs Of The Zodiac

Aries, Taurus, Gemini and Cancer,
Leo, Virgo, Libra and Scorpio,
Sagittarius, Capricorn, Aquarius and Pisces,
These are the names of the signs.

Ram, bull, twins and crab,
Lion, maiden, scales and scorpion,
Archer, goat, water-carrier and fish,
These are the things of the signs.

Mars, Venus, and Mercury,
Moon, sun and Pluto,
Jupiter, Saturn, Uranus and Neptune,
These are the planets of the signs.

Enthusiastic, practical, chatty and sensible,
Warm, logical, idealistic and intense,
Generous, down to earth, sociable and talented,
These are the qualities of the signs.

Jennifer Ingham (12)
Sir Thomas Boteler High School

Untitled

A peaceful river
Shoals of fish leaping up the
Raging waterfall.

They must try harder
Leaping higher and higher
They must reach the top.

Sophie Haddock (11)
Sir Thomas Boteler High School

The Zodiac

Aries is courageous, brave and true,
While Taurus is reliable but stubborn too.

Gemini will tell you that black is white,
And Cancer will retreat when they get a fright.

Leo says everyone, look at me,
While Virgo says please, leave me be.

Libra is the symbol of the scales,
Scorpios react strongly so look out for their tails.

Sagittarius can't wait till he is freed,
While Capricorn has a great urge to succeed.

Aquarius' views are not the normal way,
Pisces is slippery and could get away.

All of these signs are very clear,
They will see you through the year.

Ned Bibby (12)
Sir Thomas Boteler High School

Zodiac

There are twelve zodiac signs
Each with its special meaning
There's Virgo and Scorpio
The zodiac is just my thing

If it's January when you were born
You will have a star sign as common as can be
For your star sign is Capricorn
Mine personally is Virgo.

Ben Kenyon (12)
Sir Thomas Boteler High School

The Zodiac

First comes Aquarius, the water carrier, feeding the night sky
with her fulfilling water which moves through space.
Then it is Pisces, like two fish in the sea
they swim nimbly round the Earth.
Next Aries, the ram locking horns with dangerous extra terrestrials
they come within billions of miles of here.
We come to Taurus and never take this bull by the horns
or you may find yourself going intergalactic.
Here comes Gemini, identical, they say space's own twins
were made on man.
The crab Cancer is now here, so you had better watch out
because those pincers are sharp.
Then we have king of the universe, Leo the Nemean lion,
he is Aquarius' pet, protecting the water at all costs.
Virgo comes next, mother of all the galaxy.
Twins Gemini, the lover of the world, Aries' master.
Justice must follow love through and Libra decides their fate,
Heaven or Hell is its most loved choice.
Scorpio is here to stay, the only thing to kill Orion,
if you feel its sting, write your will before you die.
Sagittarius, husband of Virgo, father of Gemini,
brother of Aquarius, he shook stars with his bow.
Last is Capricorn the goat that eats space, creating black holes
and warps through space.

Ryan Edwardson (12)
Sir Thomas Boteler High School

Cancer The Crab

Crawling along the sand
Sidewalking Cancer eats fish
Snapping angrily.

Daniel Conroy (11)
Sir Thomas Boteler High School

Zodiac

All the signs are in the stars,
Some are near Mercury and some near Mars,
They can tell our fortune,
Just like my form tutor.

I like the sign Capricorn,
Because it makes me happy but mourn,
The sign for Capricorn has horns,
My mum and my cousin were born as Capricorns.

I like Sagittarius,
Because I have a friend who is a Sagittarius,
He was also very hilarious,
But very precious.

I like the sign Aquarius,
Because I am very precious,
I like the sign,
Because it makes me very happy and shine.

Toby Barnett (12)
Sir Thomas Boteler High School

What I See Poem

What I see
I see me driving the new BMW out and I'm stinking rich
I see me sitting there with no money
And driving a mini with loads of rust and doors hanging off.

Robert Herbert (12)
Sir Thomas Boteler High School

THE CRABBY CANCER CRAZE!

My shell is hard
My colour is shiny ruby
I walk sideways all day
I walk the sandy, golden bay
I live in water
With my daughter
I like to swim the sea
My family come with me
My body goes bash
As my claws go clash
I see the beautiful sea blue
I might swim right up to you
I am a vicious trancer
I am the vicious, hard Cancer.

Christopher Green (11)
Sir Thomas Boteler High School

SPACE

Different colour
Incredible, outrageous planets
Colourful alien.

Wonderful world
Shiny, shooting stars
Humungous and tiny.

Sarah Williams (11)
Sir Thomas Boteler High School

ZODIAC - CANCER

There is a cancer
Who needs an answer
He searches for miles and miles
As he walks over scratchy tiles he smiles
His white teeth shine
As he walks to number nine
As he walks through the door
He falls straight through the floor
So he climbs up the wall
And hopes to God he will not fall
As he fell
He shouted, 'Oh Hell'
And that was the end of that cancer.

Michelle Peers (12)
Sir Thomas Boteler High School

TAURUS IN SPACE

The fierce bull Taurus
Jumped into the pitch-black space
He turned and got lost

He saw many planets
And so many stars in the sky
And so bright and calm

He was so upset
He wondered how to get home
So he jumped back home.

Natasha Hughes (11)
Sir Thomas Boteler High School

The Future Of Me

What I see . . .
I was standing there with Kirsty,
We were walking into a club.
Yes . . .
It was a great day.
I was singing and dancing!
Great day.
I went to a game,
Yes . . . cool, I won.
£250 I had won.
Yeah.
I've got to win some more.
What a great day!

Ashley Stephenson (12)
Sir Thomas Boteler High School

England

I can see the world
Passing before my eyes
I see girls and boys
Growing up to be
Young men and ladies
I see shops and buildings
Opening and closing
New cars being built
New houses being built
New things happening
In this world I see
New people being born
I wonder what will happen next.

Hayley Hutchison (12)
Sir Thomas Boteler High School

GEMINI

G reat!
groovy!
great to be a mate

E xciting to
be around
when in good mood

M ad
music is one of my
favourite things

I mportant that you're not around
when I'm not in
a good mood

N ice
naughty
nocturnal

I do exciting things
I'm called
David Basford.

David Basford (12)
Sir Thomas Boteler High School

UNTITLED

Up in the sky, so high, very high
Stars and comets will fly so high
Comets and planets, stars and the moon
The moon is as white as white can be.

Joe Hatton (11)
Sir Thomas Boteler High School

Me And My Star Sign

S upportive when friends are down
A ble to do things for friends
R espectful to everyone
A nd brave and daring
H elpful and kind

My friend Rachel is Libra

L oving, kind at heart
I ntelligent, works hard for what she wants
B rave and daring, like me
R easonable in arguments too
A nd will treat everyone with respect.

Sarah Finch (12)
Sir Thomas Boteler High School

The Charming Libra

L ovely, lively, likeable and loyal,
that's what I think I am!
I ncredible, imaginative, important and indulgent,
that's what the girls think I am!
B rave, beautiful, bubbly and also bashful,
that's what my parents think I am!
R esponsible, reliable, resourceful and rational,
that's what the teachers think I am!
A rtistic, accurate, affectionate, athletic,
that's what my sister should think of me!

Geoff Wright (13)
Sir Thomas Boteler High School

THE ZODIAC

The whole of the zodiac
Is made up of star signs
That makes people what they are.

Aries: I am Dave
I am confident and quick
I will risk anything to have fun.

Virgo: My mate's name is Adam
He is diligent and shy
He will risk anything to miss school.

Pisces: My mate's name is Chris
He is sensitive and kind
Pisces will help you through your life.

That's some of the zodiac
What are you like?

David Rothwell (12)
Sir Thomas Boteler High School

SPACE IS A WORLD OF ITS OWN

The sun is a raging fire in the sky.
The moon is a custard pie.
The comets are racing balls being kicked up high.
Space is a world of its own.
Planets, stars and asteroids groan.
Rocks and rings sewn in the atmosphere.
Space is a world of its own.

Jasmine Fox (11)
Sir Thomas Boteler High School

THE VIRGO MAN

Adam is my name
Committed, loyal and true,
That's what I am.
The Virgo man through and through.
I like to do what I can,
When I can,
For who I can.
That's who I am,
The Virgo man.

The Virgo man has an active mind,
I am a pretty sensible kind of guy,
The Virgo man, that's who I am.

I am quite shy and it takes a lot for me to fly
When emotions are running high.
The Virgo man, that's who I am.

Very rarely do I lose control
But when I do, I use actions more than words.
I very rarely do.
The Virgo man, that's who I am.

Adam Hanson (13)
Sir Thomas Boteler High School

GEMINI

G roovy, great and convincing at times
E loquent, effective, joyful and always smiling
M usic and dancing are my great things
I will always be myself
N ever naughty, only when I want to be
I nfluential, youthful and witty.

Natalie Matthews (12)
Sir Thomas Boteler High School

FUTURE POEM

What I see . . .
Me driving in my big, royal blue BMW
That I won. It is lovely.
Me living in a big, white house
In the country with a big drive.

Or

Me driving down the road in a rusty banger.
Damp, mossy dump for a house
With doors hanging off the hinges.

Mikaila Peers (12)
Sir Thomas Boteler High School

WINTER'S EVENING

Winter's evening,
Stars shining through my window,
Shining through me, shine.

Winter's evening,
Moon shining up on the roof,
Shining through me, shine.

Winter's evening,
Wildlife creeping on the snow,
Creeping, creeping, crept.

Winter's evening,
It's over and gone away,
Silently at night.

Kelly Warburton (11)
Sir Thomas Boteler High School

Star Of Pisces

P recious in all ways: especially to my mum.
I mportant like the President of America:
I have to make big decisions.
S acrifice anything for anybody: definitely for my girlfriend.
C aring for anybody: especially the sick.
E xciting all the time to do lots of things: like football and tennis.
S exy and gorgeous: like my dad.

Liam Markie (12)
Sir Thomas Boteler High School

Aries

A lways caring
lways sharing
R anting on
anting to one
I am this
am that
E verything you see
verything is me
S o this is me, wink, wink, wink
o this is me, at least I think.

I hope you like this,
this is me.

I hope you like this,
as much as he.

Tony Smith (12)
Sir Thomas Boteler High School

SAGITTARIUS - AM I?

S upposed to be intellectual, fun and full of joy
A m I?
G roovy at times, am I?
I am always caring for my friends and family, am I?
T imid when something gets me down, am I?
T otally in control of my life, am I?
A lways a good friend, am I?
R ough when I want to be, am I?
I ndividually my own person, am I?
U nsure when I'm asked a question I don't know, am I?
S upposed to be all these things? I think I am!

Leah Bate (12)
Sir Thomas Boteler High School

ARIES

Aries is here, far but near
It protects the caring
It is not hard wearing
But is confident and quick
It knows every trick
It takes risks for fun
It is not scum
Also it's a very important sign
Recognisable at all times
Important and great
Eligible with no hate
Solid star sign it is.

Carrie-Anne Myles (12)
Sir Thomas Boteler High School

Leo My Life And Personality

I'm loving and caring,
Faithful and encouraging,
Happy and joyful all day round.

You can see me when I'm pleased,
But when I'm sad I'm not good to be with.
I sulk most of the day and night
Because I'm bullied all the time.

But I still love some friends to cheer me up,
They are Ben and Imran, Chris and Liam,
With me to the end.

So I'm a Leo . . . the great lion,
Who's brave and strong all day long.
But I'm too scared to use my strength,
Because I will be just as bad as the one who bullies me.

I'm very calm when it comes to the fight,
But still, I will lose.
I will not win your heart with my looks,
But happily I will win your heart with mine.

James Clarke (12)
Sir Thomas Boteler High School

Me And My Star Sign

T rusting and worthy
A ngry I may be at times
U npredictable
R anting and raving
U ltra trendy
S exy and sorted.

Kenneth Turner (11)
Sir Thomas Boteler High School

GEMINI

In space there are different star signs
Like Gemini, Scorpio, Leo and Taurus.
Geminis are very talented and witty,
They will persuade you that black is white.
The stars stay among the planets,
With Jupiter and Saturn, staying together
Like a family on string.
The stars glisten in the night
With the Plough and the Gladiator.
They all come out together, so that's zodiac.
The stars and planets as big as Earth
Come out to shine all night
And also watch the comets go by.

Benjamin Bennett (12)
Sir Thomas Boteler High School

STARS AT NIGHT

I see stars every night
Very lovely and very bright
You can do dot to dot
But sometimes you get in a knot
Then you start all over again
Drawing cats and teachers' faces
And in the morning they're not there.

Aaron Rourke (11)
Sir Thomas Boteler High School

ARIES

I am the Aries because I was born in one of its days.
I think me and my star sign mix
because I am quite risky almost every day.
In all I think of the world so much,
but I think of myself a little bit more.
It says I am confident but I am not so sure
when I am face to face with a girl.
So if I am so quick why does everyone seem to catch me?

Zead Elgaddari (12)
Sir Thomas Boteler High School

IN THE SKY

In the sky, what do I see?
Is it something good to eat?
In the sky, what do I see?
Is it something like my feet?
In the sky, what do I see?
Is it something bad to eat?
In the sky, what do I see?
Is it like a silly sheep?
In the sky, what do I see?
Is it something nice to buy?
No, it's not, it's a star,
It's just like my zodiac.

Rhiannon Rowland (12)
Sir Thomas Boteler High School

ZODIAC

The sun is a fireball,
Glowing in the sky,
Planets drift around it,
While stars twinkle by,
Meteors zoom past,
Like a formula 1 car,
Darkness is all around,
It goes on so far,
The moon is a silver balloon,
Dangling in the sky,
Astronauts land,
They jump up high.

Rachel Pickett (11)
Sir Thomas Boteler High School

THE SUN

The sun makes light
And it is normally bright,
It is like a ball of fire.
Don't forget your sunglasses,
It might burn your eyelashes.
Go to the sea,
You and me.
We'll have a laugh,
And we will be daft.

Hollie Tatlock (12)
Sir Thomas Boteler High School

PLANETS

Mercury, Venus, Earth, Mars,
Jupiter, Saturn, Uranus, Neptune,
And Pluto are all the nine planets
Of the solar system,
They are up in the sky,
Way up high,
Wish on a shooting star
And you might get a car.

Kelly Whitney (12)
Sir Thomas Boteler High School

THE MOON

The moon is like a big balloon
That in winter seems to come too soon
It leaves behind a trail of gloom
And never sees a flower bloom.

Rebecca Shaw (12)
Sir Thomas Boteler High School

UNTITLED

The roar of a lion
the heart of a man
the touch of a child
will make a lion go mad.

The ram like a lamb
will run as fast as a man
and they take time to plan.

Michael Cannons (14)
Sir Thomas Boteler High School

CANCER

C ancer people take chances with love
A nd are protective
N ever unfriendly, always kind
C heeky chatterbox and cheerful too
E ncouraging and always enjoying themselves
R elaxed, reliable and rich.

Jessica Hatton (11)
Sir Thomas Boteler High School

THE SUN

The sun is like fire,
Sun is yellow, orange, red,
Also enormous.

It is beautiful,
Golden rays of light,
Bright and burning.

Hannah Cupples (11)
Sir Thomas Boteler High School

STARS

Stars are diamonds,
Floating in the air.

Stars are fairy lights,
Twinkling by night.

Stars are genies,
Granting all your wishes.

Louise Fegan (11)
Sir Thomas Boteler High School

Capricorn Girl

I am a Capricorn.
I am very moody, obnoxious and practical.
I love to take my time.
But when someone tries to talk to me
When I'm in a mood, I go to bite their head off.

I am stroppy
When I can't get my own way.
I hate homework and get very agitated.
I love salad and cats and dogs,
Plus rabbits.

I love the word *Capricorn*
In the Chinese year I am a horse.
Beautiful, loyal, and loves dogs and monkeys,
But hates, rats and sheep.
Born in 1990
I have brill friends.

I am vicious and ferocious,
That's me. I am Verity Owen.

Verity Owen (11)
Sir Thomas Boteler High School

The Stars

The gleaming stars shoot across the night sky.
The stars are as bright as the ever burning sun.
The stars reflect in the moon's surface.
When you look at them they twinkle as bright as a silver coin.

Luke Rowe (11)
Sir Thomas Boteler High School

THE CARPET OF BLUE

Asteroids as big as our world so dear
Floating through the airless atmosphere
Millions of stars appear so clear
Against a carpet of blue so far and near
Worlds and planets gently spin
As the gravity can pull you in
A hole in the carpet shines so bright
It's called the sun, it still shines at night
Of all the planets that we know
The magic and mystery will always grow
There's lots more for us to know
So out in space we must go.

Steven Stafford (11)
Sir Thomas Boteler High School

THE SUN

The sun is bright
Shining warmth around
On the summer days.

Scarlet and golden
Like a big hot burning ball
Floating in the sky.

It's set in the sky
To let the large round moon out
Until the morning.

Rhiannon Gardner (11)
Sir Thomas Boteler High School

The Lovely Leo

Faithful and loving and encourage people
because that's the way I am

Bossy and challenging
because that's the way I am

Cheeky and funny
because that's the way I am.

Faithful, encouraging,
bossy, challenging,
cheeky,
funny and kind,
now that's the way I am.

Channelle Farrell (11)
Sir Thomas Boteler High School

Me And My Zodiac

Leo is faithful, Leo is me
Leo is encouraging, just like me.

Cancer is protective, Cancer is Josh
Take chances with love, that is Josh.

Aries is confident, Aries is quick
Aries is Daniel and he is quick.

Scorpio is mad like Leane
Compare them just like a mad man.

Jonathan Meakin (11)
Sir Thomas Boteler High School

SAGITTARIUS

S erious and sensitive
A thletic and anxious
G iving and grateful
I ntelligent and incredible
T ense and thankful
T alkative and sometimes bad tempered
A pprehensive and ace
R un as well as running races
I mperfect and impersonal
U nfortunate and uppity
S capegoat and scientific.

Katie Nichols (11)
Sir Thomas Boteler High School

STARS!

Small light in the sky
A million light years away
Tiny little dots

Small stars twinkling
A million light years away
In the midnight sky.

Small lights disappear
The night becomes brighter
The shining sun rises.

Sara Penketh (11)
Sir Thomas Boteler High School

EARTH

E very star is a symbol of a planet or comet
A far in the distance mysteriously waiting in space
R agingly spinning around
T eaching scientists so much more about things that are
H appening somewhere millions of miles away in space.

Jade Tickle (11)
Sir Thomas Boteler High School

CAPRICORN

C areful as a teacher
A nnoying like me
P erfect like my mum and dad
R anting and raving
I rritating like my brother
C onfident, golden and great
O riginal old me
R ed-hot and sexy
N utty and crazy.

Matthew Andrews (11)
Sir Thomas Boteler High School

STARS

The starry night sky
Is filled with shooting stars,
Now the dawn breaks.

The next night begins,
All of the stars are gleaming,
It's morning again.

Leah Kitchingman (11)
Sir Thomas Boteler High School

My Star Sign

A ries is confident, quick and takes big risks: that's me
R espectful to elders and teachers too! That's me
I ntelligent, brainy and always ready to give it a go: that's me
E xpected to be funny; I'm very giddy too: that's me
S turdy, hardworking and never cries: that's me.

Daniel Magill (11)
Sir Thomas Boteler High School

Scorpio

I am a Scorpio, positive and forceful
Very passionate,
Here I come.

Beware of the temper,
I'm all of these.

That's because my name is Leanne
And I'm a Scorpio.

Leanne Delooze (11)
Sir Thomas Boteler High School

Cancer!

C limbs like a monkey
A nts are my favourite animals
N ever hardly forgets anything except my homework
C rocodiles are cool!
E ats nearly everything
R uns like a leopard.

Stefan Brown (11)
Sir Thomas Boteler High School

My Treasure

I remember the first time I saw her face,
She was staring over at me.
The world around faded into nothingness,
She was all that I could see.

I remember when she came over,
I knew that it was right.
We laughed, we talked and we had fun,
Together throughout the night.

When I looked deep into her eyes,
She filled the gaping hole.
The hole that cuts deep into my heart,
When she shared with me her soul.

I remember when we first held hands,
I held her small hand quite tightly in mine.
At that moment I was beyond happiness,
I wished I could stop time.

I remember when I said to her, 'I love you,'
She cried and cried with bliss.
She whispered back, 'I love you too,'
Then we sealed our love with a kiss.

Now we are inseparable,
Rarely seen apart.
My life would be empty without her,
The girl who is in my heart.

I can't survive without her,
The rare love I treasure.
My life has no purpose without her,
Completely lacking in pleasure.

Stuart Thorniley (14)
Woolston Community High School

THE ABCs OF FRIENDSHIP

A lways looking after me.
B eing there at the right time to fulfil my needs.
C aring for me all the time.
D reams and desires of mine they always try to complete.
E nsuring my time always stays peaceful.
F orgiving me as quick as I can say 1, 2, 3.
G iving up their time *just for me.*
H eart of mine they fill with excitement.
I llnesses of mine they get rid of.
J oy they bring for me.
K eeping me warm and cosy when I am feeling cold.
L oving me more than anyone else.
M aking sure I have no problems or worries.
N ever leaving me by myself to get scared at night.
O nly worrying about me, not about themselves.
P riceless gift of theirs they have given to me but also stolen
mine (heart).
Q ueen is the word I shall use to describe the way they have
treated me.
R especting me all the time.
S upporting me every moment.
T reasuring all of their good habits in their hearts and
dumping all the bad ones in an old BMW.
U nderstanding me all the time.
V IP like looking after me.
W ishing day and night for me to get well when I am ill.
X tremely funny and humorous at times.
Y early, monthly, weekly, daily, phoning me to check if I am okay.
Z ooming to fulfil all of my needs.

Sehreen Shafaat (11)
Woolston Community High School

WHO ARE YOU?

Who are you to judge my friends
when you don't know who they are?
Who are you to judge me
when you don't even know me?

Just because I speak a different language
doesn't mean I'm wrong.

Or just because I'm not as beautiful as you
doesn't mean I'm ugly.

Or does it?

If I were black I'd be a colour
not a person, a colour.

If I were you I'd have one feeling. *Hate*.
For myself. How dare I class anyone lower than me.
I'm not better than you.
I'm not a colour, I'm not a language and
I'm not a portrait of beauty.
I'm just one girl, one person, one mind.
Now what are you?

Emma Lewis (14)
Woolston Community High School

SCHOOL DINNERS

When I'm on school dinners, believe me it's tough,
eating Brussels sprouts and all that yucky stuff.

Peas are not my strong point, I find them really gross,
I'd rather be sat at home eating egg on toast.

But my mum and dad would kill me, because they say my diet's bad,
and they put me on school dinners, so I grow up a strapping lad.

Little do my parents know, school dinners have changed a lot,
I think with all this healthy food they've really lost the plot.

While they sit there believing I'm eating carrots and asparagus tips,
I'm really sat there shovelling down a greasy burger and chips.

So thumbs up to school dinners, they've come such a long way,
no tapioca pudding like in Mum and Dad's heyday.

Sausage rolls and hot dogs, chocolate crunch to name a few,
are just some of my favourites whilst stood in the queue.

My final note is just to say school dinners are the tops,
so let's not forget who made them so, dinner ladies,
the cream of the crops.

Ashley Somma (11)
Woolston Community High School